GRADING
SMARTER

NOT HARDER

**Assessment Strategies That Motivate
Kids and Help Them Learn**

ASCD MEMBER BOOK

Many ASCD members received this book as a
member benefit upon its initial release.

Learn more at: **www.ascd.org/memberbooks**

GRADING
SMARTER
NOT HARDER

Assessment Strategies That Motivate Kids and Help Them Learn

MYRON DUECK

ASCD | Alexandria, VA USA

1703 N. Beauregard St. • Alexandria, VA 22311-1714 USA
Phone: 800-933-2723 or 703-578-9600 • Fax: 703-575-5400
Website: www.ascd.org • E-mail: member@ascd.org
Author guidelines: www.ascd.org/write

Gene R. Carter, *Executive Director;* Richard Papale, *Acting Chief Program Development Officer;* Stefani Roth, *Interim Publisher;* Genny Ostertag, *Acquisitions Editor;* Julie Houtz, *Director, Book Editing & Production;* Ernesto Yermoli, *Editor;* Lindsey Smith, *Senior Graphic Designer;* Mike Kalyan, *Manager, Production Services;* Cynthia Stock, *Typesetter;* Andrea Wilson, *Production Specialist*

PAPERBACK ISBN: 978-1-4166-1890-4   ASCD product # 114003   8A/14
Quantity discounts: 10–49, 10%; 50+, 15%; 1,000+, special discounts (e-mail programteam@ascd.org or call 800-933-2723, ext. 5773, or 703-575-5773). Also available in e-book formats. For desk copies, go to www.ascd.org/deskcopy.

ASCD Member Book No. FY14-8A (July 2014 PSI+). ASCD Member Books mail to Premium (P), Select (S), and Institutional Plus (I+) members on this schedule: Jan, PSI+; Feb, P; Apr, PSI+; May, P; Jul, PSI+; Aug, P; Sep, PSI+; Nov, PSI+; Dec, P. For current details on membership, see www.ascd.org/membership.

Library of Congress Cataloging-in-Publication Data

Dueck, Myron.
   Grading smarter, not harder : assessment strategies that motivate kids and help them learn / Myron Dueck.
      pages cm.
   Includes bibliographical references and index.
      ISBN 978-1-4166-1890-4 (pbk. : alk. paper) 1. Educational tests and measurements—United States.
   2. Grading and marking (Students)—United States. 3. Educational evaluation—United States. I. Title.
      LB3051.D668 2014
      371.26—dc23
                                                                            2014009519

23 22 21 20 19   5 6 7 8 9 10 11 12

GRADING SMARTER
NOT HARDER

**Assessment Strategies That Motivate
Kids and Help Them Learn**

Select figures from this book can be downloaded at
www.ascd.org/ascd/pdf/books/dueck2014figures.pdf

To Elijah and Sloane—keep learning, keep exploring.

In memory of Diane.

ACKNOWLEDGMENTS

Writing a book was more of a challenge than I could have ever imagined. Though the process takes hundreds of hours spent in quiet contemplation, much of the final product is due to the contributions and guidance of others. It is with incredible gratitude that I take the time to acknowledge them here.

Students: Students have provided me with invaluable feedback and the opportunity to continue my quest to be a better educator. I thank you for your honesty, your criticism, and your willingness to try something new; without you, none of my work would have mattered at all. I am especially grateful to the at-risk learners—many of whom I mention in this book—who, despite feeling vulnerable, take on the challenge of learning.

Educators: The tough questions provided by educators have undoubtedly helped me to better understand and articulate the complexities, challenges, and solutions related to grading and assessment. A special thanks to those educators in both Canada and the United States who contributed templates or ideas discussed in this book: Ben Arcuri, Shona Becker, Chris Bradley, Scott Harkness, Karl Koehler, Cindy Postlethwaite, Russ Reid, Doug Scotchburn, Naryn Searcy, Chris Terris, Geoff Waterman, and Lisa West. Over the past seven years, School District 67 in British Columbia has provided me a wealth of opportunities, and I am very fortunate to have such incredible colleagues.

Assessment Leaders: A number of people have been instrumental to my grading and assessment journey. Ken O'Connor—you have provided the solutions to the problem of broken grades and paved the way to amassing credible data related to standards-based assessment; thank you for being a friend, mentor, and sounding board for me on many occasions. Your willingness to write the foreword to this book leaves me indebted. Rick Stiggins—you are an assessment icon and you have established the benchmark for continuing the conversation on grading and assessment. Jan Chappuis, Jacob Bruno, and the rest of the Assessment Training Institute team—your conferences and training have provided a stage upon which educators can continually hold meaningful discussions on grading and assessment. Tom Schimmer—you played an absolutely critical role in starting me down the path toward sound assessment, and your suggestion that I write down the feedback from my students was arguably the best advice I ever received. Without your leadership at Princess Margaret and your willingness to engage in tough conversations, I just can't see how I would have ventured this deep into the assessment conversation. If your challenge to other educators is as effective for them as it was for me, your impact on assessment will be global.

School Leaders: Bill Bidlake—thank you for providing opportunity and support for educators willing to take risks. Terry Grady and Don MacIntyre—thank you for being incredible mentors and for providing a venue for my comments when I felt most frustrated. Wendy Hyer—thanks for the professional and personal support in my growth as a leader both inside and beyond our school district.

Book Production: Dianne Hildebrand—you taught me English in 12th grade, and who would have thought you would come to my rescue in the process of editing my book? Genny Ostertag and Ernesto Yermoli at ASCD—I couldn't have asked for better people to guide me through my first book. Your feedback and direction are what made this book go from a collection of thoughts to a finished product—thank you!

Friends: Chris Van Bergeyk and Todd Manuel—your constant moral support, questions, and thoughts through the writing of this book were more helpful than you realize. Russ Reid and Cindy Postlethwaite—thank you for being the two teachers to whom I could run for reassurance when I needed it most. Jeremy Hiebert—thanks for reminding me that a mountain bike ride makes for a great educational conversation. Ben Arcuri—your unabashed honesty and eye for criticism has kept me on track many times. Thanks for the support and your authentic approach to educational confrontation. You personify the saying, "Growth comes from being surrounded by critical friends."

Family: Diane—thank you for showing me that the value of taking on a challenge is not measured by win or loss, but by the way in which we tackle it. You were one of my strongest supporters, and I wish I could have shared the completion of this project with you. Ben—thanks for mentoring me on divergent thinking and looking at situations from an angle not yet considered. Dad—thanks for decades of instilling in me the belief that no problem is without a solution. Mom—thanks for showing me how to care for others, and also for the piano lessons; I am now able to sit and work for hours even though I would rather be doing something else. Kev—thanks for a lifetime of fun, debate, reflection, and challenges. And finally, Tracey, Elijah, and Sloane—you provide me with ample support and honest feedback, and for that I am eternally grateful. Elijah and Sloane, you have taught me much about different learning characteristics, as well as what works and what doesn't when it comes to motivation and consequences. Thank you for being both understanding and patient while "Daddy works on his book." Tracey, I do not have enough words to express my thanks. This assessment journey is not what you signed up for, but your never-ending support has made it so much easier. Thank you for being my partner and friend.

FOREWORD

Have you read books that made you both laugh and cry? How often can you say this about a book on assessment and grading? My guess is that for most educators, the answer is along the following lines: "You have to be joking—assessment and grading are serious aspects of teaching and learning. Books on those topics affect me professionally and intellectually, not emotionally." But professional content that affects us emotionally provides us with a deeper sense of connection to it and is far more likely to have a positive influence on our professional beliefs and practices.

This book made me both laugh and cry. I wish I had been able to read it 47 years ago, before I began my first year of teaching. The stories Myron tells about teachers and students speak powerfully both to the positive effects that assessment and grading can have when they are done well and to the negative effects that ensue when they are done badly. Sadly, the latter is true for most traditional approaches to assessment and grading.

In many ways, Myron's path reflects my own journey from rookie teacher to classroom veteran to consultant on assessment and grading. Fortunately for Myron and his students, his epiphanies and resulting changes to practice have happened while he is still in the classroom; unfortunately for me and my students, most of my epiphanies happened after I had left the classroom. Please don't get the wrong idea—I believe that I was a good teacher most of the time, but thanks more to an intuitive sense of what's good teaching and what's good for learning than to any teacher preparation program or professional development course. As I see it, one of the biggest problems with teacher education programs is the lack of courses on assessment and grading. Even when such courses are available, they are often not required for graduation and they rarely include any information about grading. Until recently, the same has been true of most in-service professional development offerings. In either a preparatory or professional-development context, *Grading Smarter, Not Harder* should be required reading. Not only is it well referenced and research based, it is also fun to read and practical.

Myron makes it clear that the journey to productive assessment and grading is not easy and sometimes involves missteps, so teachers should have the confidence to go outside their comfort zone to make changes that are good for students. As Myron makes clear in this book, changes need to be good not only for all learners, but for teachers as well.

Grading Smarter, Not Harder allows teachers to reflect on their own successes and failures and to understand the solutions that Myron suggests. There is so much good advice in this book that I am not going to try to summarize the whole thing, but I will identify four key lessons that stood out for me:

1. **Teachers should grade smarter, not harder.** Though teachers frequently complain that student-centered assessment for learning places unreasonable demands on their time, Myron

points out that by working smarter, teachers can actually diminish their workloads.

2. **We are often better coaches than teachers.** Myron discusses the importance of applying coaching skills learned on the playing field to the classroom. When I coached field hockey, I looked for things I could do that would move us to the next level of performance—in effect, assessment of learning.

3. **Learning is more important than grades.** Traditional practice is to grade everything students do regardless of its purpose. As Myron points out, if we organize our lessons according to learning goals and identify clear levels of performance, the focus remains on learning; advice on how to improve naturally follows.

4. **Relationships are crucial.** As Myron notes, changes to assessment practice can affect not only the relationships among teachers and students, but also those among students and parents and students and their peers. Positive relationships are the sine qua non for success in teaching and learning.

Myron is a valued personal and professional friend, so I was pleased and honored when he asked me to write the foreword for this book. It has been an absolute joy to watch him progress from a participant at ATI conferences in Portland to a presenter at those conferences and at other places around the world. I am so glad that Myron wrote this book because now an even wider audience will be able to benefit from his journey and the wise advice that he gives. Thank you, Myron.

Ken O'Connor
Scarborough (not Toronto), Ontario
February 2014

INTRODUCTION

At the early age of 19, my dad was given control of a house-moving crew by his father. He went on to spend over 20 years figuring out how to move structures from one place to another. The process of moving buildings does not lend itself to standardization: invariably, each move involves many unforeseen challenges that must be surmounted before a structure can be trundled down the road—if there *is* a road, and sometimes there isn't. Dueck Building Movers has transported dwellings across frozen lakes in the winter and by barge in the summer.

Often, my dad would agree to a project first and figure out the logistics later—clearly, he was a problem solver. Thanks to my dad's influence, I grew up knowing that "it won't work" was never an adequate response to a situation if all avenues hadn't first been thoroughly explored. This mind-set proved helpful when I first encountered the concepts of sound grading practices and assessment for learning

(AFL). Many of my colleagues voiced their concerns about these new approaches:

- "The ideas will never work in content-heavy high school courses."
- "I would never try these reckless changes in courses that have mandated standardized exams."
- "Getting rid of late penalties and zeros will result in a slide toward irresponsibility and chaos."

Despite the warnings, I forged ahead with changing some of the grading and assessment routines in my class. Initially, I found these shifts daunting and was tempted to return to more familiar assessment methods. But I stuck with the changes, and—like my father—solved any problems as they arose. Six years later, I have revolutionized the way I collect, tabulate, and present the grades of my students. I have also incorporated assessment routines that promote learning rather than merely (and inaccurately) measure it. Instead of sliding into the inevitable chaos that so many people predicted, I have found the following to be true:

- My students' scores on government-mandated tests have steadily risen.
- My students' grades more accurately reflect their understanding of government-mandated learning outcomes.
- My students feel more connected to the grading and assessment systems in my classroom.
- My grading techniques are fairer and more equitable than before.
- I have formed stronger, more sustainable relationships with my students.
- Students exhibit a heightened level of ownership, responsibility, and accountability in my classes.
- I have been able to explore more effective interventions for at-risk students than before.

We replicate the systems from which we advance, which is arguably the biggest reason why schools continue to keep one foot entrenched in the Industrial Age. Virtually any staffwide conversation on student grading includes arguments for enforcing rigor, responsibility, and hard work. Missing assignments receive no credit because "nothing equals zero" and mistakes are met with penalties. Support for maintaining a school's traditional grading and assessment policies may be as deeply rooted as the trees on school grounds. Changes to allow for retesting are met with particular resistance, with many educators firm in their belief that "students should get it right the first time" and teachers who re-assess students often seen as "soft."

Fortunately, teachers who embrace a more personalized approach to assessment have plenty of support. In his book *World Class Learners* (2012), Yong Zhao compares traditional education systems to sausage making, noting that we have taken individual interests, goals, and attributes and dumped them all in the same grinder (school system) to churn out identical sausages (students). Though we may have needed a lot of uniformly educated workers back in the Industrial Age, this is no longer the case. In a recent interview with *The New York Times,* Laszlo Bock, senior vice president for operations at Google, made this point plainly:

> One of the things we've seen from all our data crunching is that GPAs are worthless as criteria for hiring, and test scores are worthless. . . . After two or three years, your ability to perform at Google is completely unrelated to how you performed when you were in school. . . . You want people who like figuring out stuff where there is no obvious answer. (Bryant, 2013)

Even those at the very top of our educational and innovative food chain recognize that the landscape has shifted away from task-oriented information processing. Lawrence Summers, the former president of Harvard University, says that "increasingly, anything you learn is going to become obsolete within a decade and so the most important kind of learning is about how to learn" (Bradshaw, 2012). There is ample support outside of K–12 schools for changing the traditional model of education, but change does not come easy.

The Process

This book is a detailed account of how and why I came to change my approach to grading and assessing students. Once I felt confident that the changes I had introduced were effective, I shared some of them with colleagues, many of whom were quick to inform me that there were no second chances in the "real world" and that my acceptance of retesting would hurt students and the community. Other educators challenged my decision to stop grading uniform homework assignments; they were convinced that students simply wouldn't do ungraded homework. However, as nebulous speculation gave way to concrete student accounts of success, it became increasingly difficult for anyone to discount the effectiveness of my approach. Students were gaining more confidence, and at-risk learners were passing courses in which the grading was outcome-based.

Decades of research point to indisputable evidence that grading penalties are far less effective than feedback and personalized learning. Responsive teaching has always reacted to the needs of learners over the agendas of teachers: it is less about delivering a grade than about delivering timely, accurate, and specific feedback (Reeves, 2010).

As I developed my new approach to grading and assessment, two items in particular influenced me greatly: Ken O'Connor's *A Repair Kit for Grading: 15 Fixes for Broken Grades* (2010), which challenged me to examine the methods by which I graded my students and the extent to which my routines measured student learning; and Rick Stiggins's three essential questions that students should always be able to answer (Where am I going? Where am I now? How can I close the gap?; Chappuis and colleagues, 2012).

Effect on Learners

If my father's experiences as a building mover influenced me when I first tackled changes to grading and assessment, my mother's experiences as a nurse seem to influence me more six years later. At her job, my mom formed relationships that were strengthened by the fact that everyone involved wanted to do well, feel well, and better themselves. People want to feel a sense of confidence—both in themselves and in the systems upon which they rely. The reality is that some people need help attaining this.

Confidence is critical to learning, and my students have demonstrated an increase in confidence since I started making changes. They now feel empowered by the opportunity to meaningfully engage in their own learning and improve as lifelong learners. All educators can personalize learning and see the power of increased student confidence, but we need concrete examples of and structures for how best to achieve this. In this book you'll find a number of strategies that have increased student confidence in my classroom.

In addition to grading and assessment routines, it is important for teachers to be aware of socioeconomic issues affecting students. My mom's work as a nurse involved caring for the disadvantaged and extending extra assistance to those who most needed it—actions that influenced me when, as a teacher, I noticed how much greater obstacles to learning were for students living with poverty than for their affluent peers. The unmistakable effects of poverty on student achievement are a grading issue: although some students are at a greater disadvantage than others, we tend to grade all our students using the same criteria. This approach too often deepens the academic frustration of at-risk learners and gravely misrepresents the extent to which these students understand the content. It's been my experience that alternative approaches to grading, testing, and homework can actually improve the academic standing and disposition of impoverished students. The same is true for students who are under immense pressure to excel: when the window through which such students can demonstrate their skills widens, anxiety subsides and accountability increases.

Criteria for Punitive Action: The CARE Guidelines

I have developed what I call the CARE guidelines—four requirements that must be met before I apply classroom penalties to students:

- **Care:** The student must *care* about the consequences of the penalty.
- **Aims:** The results of the penalty must complement my overall *aims* as a teacher.
- **Reduction:** The penalty must result in a *reduction* of the negative behavior.
- **Empowerment:** The student must feel *empowered* regarding the actions for which he or she is being penalized.

These four conditions have fundamentally altered the way I mete out penalties in school.

A Leap of Faith

One of my favorite movie scenes of all time is found in *Indiana Jones and the Last Crusade.* Near the end of the film, Indiana Jones is faced with the last of three challenges: the leap of faith. As he stands at the edge of a deep chasm, he is forced to step forward to what appears to be a certain death. Indiana Jones closes his eyes, takes a deep breath, and steps forward—only to find that he is stepping onto a bridge that he had been unable to see. Over the past six years, I've had to take many of my own leaps of faith, stepping away from the familiar and toward the uncertain. I had to trust the research that supported the changes I was making and have the courage to question my own long-held beliefs. And unlike Indiana Jones, I had the luxury of simply returning back to what I had been doing before if my changes didn't work out.

I suggest that the uncertain reader take a path similar to mine. Try one thing from this book that appears to have merit. Adapt it to suit the grade level and subject you are teaching. Inform your students of the new process and let them know that you are as much a learner in the process as they are. Finally, with an honest and open frame of mind, observe the effects that the change has on your class. If the change works, keep doing it and consider trying something else as well. Write down your experiences and note the feedback you receive from students. Who knows? You might write a book about it one day.

1

GRADING

Imagine you're a student on the first day of class. In reviewing the class norms and expectations, your teacher addresses the issue of bathroom breaks as follows:

> Although we all know you should use the bathroom during your break so that you don't interrupt my teaching or your learning, you will each receive five tokens that you can use throughout the semester whenever "nature calls" during class. Once you have exhausted your five tokens, you will be deducted 1 percent of your grade at the end of the course for each additional time that you use the bathroom during class. Because I believe in fairness, the converse will be true as well: for every token you have left over at the end of the course, I will add 1 percent to your final grade.

I hope that very few educators would agree that bathroom visits should be tied to measures of learning outcomes! An online search for "frequent urination" should convince even the most steadfast supporter of this token system that someone who needs to use the bathroom frequently is probably not doing so by choice. Pregnancy, bladder infection, stress, diabetes, and a host of other conditions can cause someone to have to urinate frequently.

To what extent do members of the educational community introduce nonacademic variables into the grading of student learning? How many of these variables lie outside of students' direct control? These two questions will help guide the conversation in this chapter.

Behaviors Versus Academics

Let's examine some hypothetical scenarios that involve missing student assignments. For each scenario, let's assume we know the intricate details of each student's experience and ability.

Scenario 1: Tim is walking to school with a completed science assignment safely secured in his backpack when a thief suddenly accosts him and forces him to surrender his backpack. Is the fact that Tim arrives at school without his homework a measure of his learning or ability? Clearly, the answer is no. If any measure were to be applied here, it would be of his bad luck or poor choice of school route.

Scenario 2: Sally chooses not to bother even starting her science assignment, though she's a very capable student and would likely do well on it. In this instance, is the absence of an assignment a measure of learning or ability? Again, the answer would be no: because Sally did not complete it, her teacher can't measure its merit. If any measure were to be applied here, it would be of her stubbornness or poor decision making.

Scenario 3: Lee is new to his school, having moved into town with his family a few months ago. He struggles with his English speaking and writing skills. He has no friends at school and remains very quiet in class, sitting by himself and seldom asking for help. Though he misses the due date for his science assignment, his teacher can't determine whether or not he is able to complete it because he is so quiet. The fact is that Lee, uncertain of his ability to complete the assignment, never even starts it. His weak English skills make it hard for him to convey what little understanding he has on the subject. Is Lee's lack of work a measure of learning or ability? Although his choice not even to try completing the assignment is a behavioral decision, it is partly due to a lack of linguistic confidence and a fear of failure. An academic measure might be applied in this case, but determining it would be very difficult.

Scenario 4: Clark tries to complete his science assignment but gives up in frustration. He crumples it up and throws it in the garbage. When his mom demands that he take the assignment out of the trash and complete it, Clark dumps her coffee on it, slams the front door, and goes off to hang out with his buddies at the skate park. Although this scenario is the closest to allowing for a measure of academic ability, there is no evidence available of Clark's level of understanding, and it is unlikely that anyone is willing to sift through the city landfill to find it.

I decided a few years ago that I would only measure hard evidence of the extent to which students understood and could meet established learning goals. To be clear, the behaviors my students exhibit in class and throughout the school are very important to me. As educators, we must preserve and guard our role in forming and encouraging positive behaviors among young people. That said, I have chosen to make every attempt to avoid factoring student behaviors into my grading unless I am explicitly asked to do so by prescribed learning outcomes. Fairly applied, this approach must go both ways: if we decide not to penalize students for negative behaviors, then conversely we should not inflate grades on account of positive ones.

Ultimately, behaviors will factor into grading whether or not we explicitly attempt to measure them. Students who show up to class on time, arrive with the necessary materials, attempt to complete their homework, and treat others nicely will likely benefit academically—just as students who make poor decisions will suffer academically. If teachers make every effort to collect evidence of learning and measure this alone, behaviors will result in their logical consequences. As my friend and colleague Chris Terris put it, "I care far more about my son's behavior indicators than I do about his academic grade; if he is trying hard, paying attention, and doing what he is supposed to, his grade will fall where it belongs."

"Lates" and Zeros

When addressing punitive grading measures in this chapter, I will be speaking mainly of *deductions for late assignments* ("*lates*") and *zeros*. Any discussion of zeros must include a distinction between a 4-point scale and 100-point scale. Doug Reeves (2010) explains the difference very well:

> On a four-point scale, where "A" = "4," "B" = "3," and so on, the zero is accurate, because the difference between the "A," "B," "C," "D," and "F" are all equal—one point. But assigning a zero on a 100-point scale is a math error; it implies a 60-point difference between the "D" and "F," while the other differences are typically about 10 points. It makes missing a single assignment the "academic death penalty." It's not just unfair—it is not mathematically accurate. (p. 78)

The majority of the zeros I see getting handed out are on a 100-point scale. Both lates and zeros are attempts to affect behavior by statistically incorporating punitive measures into the grading scheme.

Here are some examples of how lates and zeros are typically used in grading decisions:

- 10 percent of the grade is deducted per day after the assignment's due date.
- A 50 percent deduction is applied to the assignment following an arbitrary number of days beyond the original due date.

- After the due date, the assignment is graded on a pass/fail basis; if awarded a "pass," 50 percent of the grade is still deducted.
- If the assignment is not handed in by the due date, it receives an automatic zero.

Other grading schemes incorporate penalties in less obvious ways. Here are a few such examples I have encountered:

- A teacher gives a quiz as soon as class begins, and anyone who arrives late is not allowed to take the quiz. Any student who does not take the quiz is given a zero. As a result, students who arrive late to class receive a grade based entirely on their lack of punctuality on a quiz designed to measure learning.
- The top aggregate score a student can have on a summative unit test is reduced based on the number of missing assignments or homework tasks during that unit—so, for example, if Sally only completes 80 percent of the homework assignments, the maximum score she can receive on the unit test is 80 percent.
- Missed tests are given a zero unless students agree to attend a mandatory tutorial session. The session is offered at 6 p.m. on Friday evenings and must be booked via written application two weeks in advance. The make-up test is administered one week after the tutorial—also at 6 p.m. on Friday. Because of the rigidity and inconvenience of this "tutorial support," very few students go through with it.

The Four Conditions for Punitive Action

Penalties should be just, reasonable, and linked as closely as possible to the offense if the threat of their enactment is to effectively change behaviors. Here's an example. As a young car driver, I received a lot of speeding tickets. Paying over $1,200 in fines, though inconvenient, did little to curb my speeding habit. What eventually compelled me to lay off the accelerator was a meeting I had at the government-licensing branch. "One more ticket in the next 365 days, Mr. Dueck, and you will have your license suspended for one year," proclaimed the humorless adjudicator. That is all it took for me to go from being pulled over four times a year to getting pulled over once every four years. The threat of losing my license for a year worked well to modify my behavior because it met the CARE guidelines mentioned in the introduction to this book:

- **Care:** The prospect of not being allowed to drive my car for a year terrified me. To say that I cared would be a massive understatement.
- **Aims:** The government wants safer roads and fewer emergency calls. Speeding drivers should pay for the costs that they incur.
- **Reduction:** Since that meeting in 1994, I have had three speeding infractions and I have never been summoned for another licensing meeting.
- **Empowerment:** I had power over my own speeding and it was up to me to slow down. Only I could improve my time management, leave earlier for important events, and turn on the cruise control feature.

Where the threat of losing my driver's license met the CARE guidelines for punitive action, behavior-based grading does not. Here is why.

Care

Many students do not appear to care about grading consequences. Consider the following conversation I had with a frustrated educator who used late penalties:

Teacher: I use late penalties of 10 to 20 percent reductions and I will tell you why: I am tired of working harder than my students. I put in the effort, the time at lunch or after school, and they don't.

Me: I have felt the same frustration. Do most of these students seem to care about a 10 or 20 percent deduction to their grades?

Teacher: (Pause.) No, and that is a huge frustration as well. I keep applying the same penalty to the same students.

Some students care about grading penalties and others don't. Those who are very concerned about getting into a good college might work hard to avoid grading penalties, whereas others might prefer to suffer the penalties than to actually complete their assignments. Students who ask questions like "If I don't hand in my work, what is my grade going to be?" or "If I get a zero on this assignment, am I still passing?" are probably debating whether or not to consider the assignment optional. When students opt to ignore assignments, penalties may serve to make teachers feel as though they've addressed the issue, but they do not increase student accountability or responsibility. Academic threats have lost their potency for students who are already disillusioned with their school experience and thus inclined to think, "If I'm already failing, why should I care about another zero?" Many students confront issues that loom much larger than late or missing assignments.

For many years I handed out penalties for late assignments like they were candy. It took me too long to recognize that school is like society at large: if we are building more prisons, something isn't working.

Aims

Punitive grading does not complement my overall aim to measure learning outcomes, increase student confidence, and provide an environment of fairness and equity. My job requires me to measure evidence of learning or capacity against a set of standards. If my grades reflect behavioral penalties, then they do not relate directly to learning outcomes. Furthermore, applying lates and zeros does not inspire academic confidence in my students, some of whom may be very capable academically but struggling with behavior patterns. And despite popular belief, punitive grades diminish fairness and equity in the classroom: the moment I apply grading consequences to factors outside my classroom, some students will be penalized more than others for factors that are not in their control.

Reduction

Punitive grading may not result in a reduction of the negative behavior. Consider, for example, that an estimated 20 percent of people are chronic procrastinators (Marano, 2003). Students in this cohort who have trouble meeting deadlines and who struggle with organization will undoubtedly feel frustrated and discouraged by lates and zeros. (I can speak from experience as someone who struggles with punctuality and due dates—traits directly linked to my speeding violations.)

Many systems in our society account for the fact that humans will predictably miss deadlines. Airlines appear to set the boarding time for the flight further in advance than is actually required; the state of Iowa has a 60-day grace period for those who forget to renew their driver's licenses on or before their birthdays. Those who think teachers are all punctual and time-conscious might be disappointed at the reality that many teachers struggle with due dates. In every school in which I've worked, a certain percentage of teachers tended to arrive late for staff meetings. I do not know if they were penalized for this, and I am not suggesting that they should have been; for all I know, these teachers were late because they were helping students or giving injured athletes first aid.

Empowerment

Students being penalized must have power over the causational variables. Of the four conditions that must be satisfied in order for me to apply a penalty, this is arguably the most powerful. As Ross Greene (2009) puts it, we have to believe that "if a kid could do well, he would do well" (p. 49). Many of the factors that affect students' abilities to succeed in school lie outside of their control. Here are some examples:

Poverty. Around 22 percent of students in the United States live in poverty (Felling, 2013; National Poverty Center, 2013). Many of them lack basic amenities such as electricity, heat, and access to computers or the Internet, and face such additional hurdles as utility disconnection, depression, overcrowded homes, and physical abuse (Jensen, 2009). Because nobody chooses to be poor, any of the effects of poverty that contribute to students' lates and zeros in school are by definition outside of their control.

Ability. Student may not have the ability to complete certain assignments, whether because of learning disabilities, gaps in learning due to school transfers, health issues, inadequate mentoring, truancy, or lack of background knowledge.

Confidence. Lack of confidence can prevent students from even attempting assignments, or cause them to surrender at the first sign of difficulty. Such students may find it easier to avoid their work entirely than to take another hit to their self-esteem, and may also lack the confidence to ask for help. Such negative patterns can extend over generations, as the inability to self-advocate is often an inherited trait (Gladwell, 2008).

Environment. Students from lower-income families are more likely to live in households where violence or neglect is present, or that are simply exceptionally loud or busy (Jensen, 2009). Many students wait until late in the evening, when the likelihood that arguments or other disturbances will erupt wanes dramatically, to complete their homework.

Substance abuse and emotional struggles. Concentration and ability can be severely inhibited by drug and alcohol issues and by emotional struggles due to conflict, isolation, or neglect. Research indicates that success in math and languages is most adversely affected by students' emotional states (Medina, 2008).

Parents. As both a teacher and an administrator, I have witnessed the positive and negative effects of parenting decisions. In many cases, parents enable negative student behaviors by excusing their children's truancy. Conversely, some parents will refuse to excuse their children when they skip a test, thus flinging open the door to all of the grading penalties at the teacher's disposal. Such differences in parenting affect both to whom and to what extent penalties are levied.

Many educators still hold on to the assumption that parents are capable, grounded, and in control of their children. Add this to the list of traditional mind-sets in need of an overhaul. Too often, children are more capable than their parents, often attempting to balance school-work with raising younger siblings, buying groceries, and masking their parents' substance abuse and violence issues.

How Behavior-Based Grading Contributes to Statistical Sabotage

If a student makes a concerted effort to complete a quiz and does not get a single answer correct, then a zero grade is arguably an accurate measure of the student's understanding. However, if the student receives a zero simply because he or she didn't complete the quiz, then the grade is not an accurate measure of understanding (O'Connor, 2010). Once the accuracy of grading data is compromised, a number of difficulties emerge.

Imagine a scenario in which Johnny is scheduled to take two quizzes for the same class, one on Monday and the other on Thursday. He skips the Monday quiz but is present for the one on Thursday. Johnny's teacher gives him an automatic zero on Monday's quiz because he didn't take it, and a zero on Thursday's quiz because he got all the answers wrong. Anyone looking at the teacher's grade book would find it impossible to determine whether the zeros reflect lack of work or lack of understanding. If Johnny also receives lates on assignments, his grading data are even more ambiguous. The teacher in this case might be advised to use special codes or symbols to understand and possibly defend Johnny's aggregate score. I will admit to having had the following type of conversation in parent-teacher meetings:

Me: Good afternoon, Ms. Smith. Thanks for attending the parent-teacher conference.

Ms. Smith: Thanks. My daughter Jill is really struggling in social studies. I was devastated to see that she got 55 percent on her report card.

Me: Well, perhaps she's not doing that badly.

Ms. Smith: What do you mean? Is she not at 55 percent?

Me (pausing, showing some discomfort): Well, I can see that, in my grade book, some of her scores are circled in blue and others are highlighted. Those symbols indicate a reduction in value from what she would have had if she had handed the work in on time.

Ms. Smith: I'm confused.

Me: Well, um, one circle indicates that the assignment was a day late and therefore the score would have been 10 percent greater than it is. Two circles means that the assignment was two days late and therefore would have been 20 percent greater. I see here that I used a highlighter over the top of the existing circles for her poster assignment, indicating that the score was reduced more than 30 percent—most likely to a maximum of 50 percent.

Ms. Smith: Most likely?

Me (deciding to switch tactics): Listen, if Jill would get her work in on time, we wouldn't be having this confusion.

Ms. Smith: Confusion is right. I wish I had known about all of these lates. Did you phone or e-mail me about these issues?

Me: Sorry, I guess I should have called, but I can't keep up with all of these lates in each of my classes and it is Jill's responsibility to let you know.

Ms. Smith: Do you think most teenagers will come home and tell their parents about late or missing assignments?

Me: Probably not.

Ms. Smith: I guess I just want to know where she is actually at academically and to know that 55 percent means something.

I have come to agree with parents like Ms. Smith. She does have the right to know her daughter's actual grade standing according to the learning outcomes.

Imagine the confusion and frustration that would occur if this type of punitive measurement system were used in the medical community—for example, if a patient's overdue hospital parking fine were factored into her blood pressure reading. It's a challenge to find any other profession that purports to offer personal, measurable data in which the numbers can be as warped as we allow them to be in education.

It is disturbing that the destructive power of a zero grade is often the reason that teachers use it. If the goal is to punish or compel, a zero is the ultimate numerical weapon. When factored into the average of an otherwise consistent set of scores, the result can be considerable. Consider the examples in Figure 1.1, showing two sets of identical scores except for a single zero. As a measure of learning, 59.6 percent

Figure 1.1
Effect of a Zero Score on the Final Average (Example 1)

Scores	Scores
78	78
71	71
74	0
68	68
81	81
Final Average	**Final Average**
74.4	59.6

is clearly a misrepresentation of the extent to which the student likely understands the material. A serious statistical problem exists if we assume that the rest of the scores are based on sound assessments. None of the scores making up the 59.6 percent average come close to the mean score. The whole point of determining an average is to arrive at a singular representation of a set of numbers.

Clearly, zeros can blur the extent to which students demonstrate improvement or mastery of the material. Consider the set of scores in Figure 1.2, purporting to represent tennis-serving skills measured over the course of a two-week unit. The conclusion that the student

Figure 1.2
Effect of a Zero Score on the Final Average (Example 2)

Successful Serves (Out of 10)
March 1:   0
March 2:   0
March 3:   0
March 4:   2
March 5:   3
March 8:   5
March 9:   7
March 10: 8
March 11: 8
March 12: 9
Average: 4.2/10

properly completed roughly 4 out of 10 serves is not accurate and in no way predicts future performance. If any of the non-zero scores have further been reduced for reasons not directly pertaining to her tennis-serving skills, such as for tardiness or talking out of turn, then the ambiguity of the scores is even further compounded.

Let's assume that Catherine, a high school sophomore, attends only half of her biology classes during a two-week unit on communicable diseases. On the day of the summative unit test, Catherine opts to skip class and go for coffee with her girlfriends instead. On account of her truancy, she gets a zero on the test. What are the chances that Catherine, at age 16, knows something about herpes, mononucleosis, or AIDS? If Catherine knows absolutely nothing about communicable diseases by the end of the unit, she has either been living under a rock for most of her life or her teacher is completely incompetent. Any score above zero would far more accurately represent the degree of Catherine's knowledge.

Growing up, I had a toy version of NASCAR legend Richard Petty's racecar—number 43. If we are after grades that accurately measure student understanding, adopting a policy of using the numbers of students' favorite racecars for missing work would make about as much sense as using zeros.

Strategies for Addressing Uncompleted Work

Following are some possible solutions for ensuring that student grades more accurately measure

PERSONAL STORY

Imagine that the history teachers at Colonial High School are so fed up with their students' late and missing assignments that they appropriate their department's budget to pay for a set of wooden stocks such as those used in colonial times to punish wrongdoers. Not only do the stocks serve to teach students a little history, but they also help motivate students to complete their work on time. The teachers institute a simple rule: get your assignments in by the due date or spend a day in the stocks. The students, terrified at the prospect of being constrained in a wooden device and having tomatoes pelted at them by jeering classmates, all begin delivering their assignments on time. To their delight, the teachers hardly ever need to resort to the stocks. The system is considered a resounding success: very few students are punished, and rates of homework completion skyrocket.

The history teachers throw a party at the house of the mastermind behind the idea, Mr. Bastille. Though Ms. Lamb, the head of the science department, can hear the revelry from her house down the street, she is not feeling the celebratory zeal. She is frustrated because many of her own students have suddenly stopped handing in their work on time, choosing to spend their time on history assignments instead. Though she's unaware of the history teachers' newly instituted method of punishment, she has overheard some of her students discussing stocks and is surprised at their newfound interest in economics.

If this story were to continue, the science teachers would either ask the history teachers to dismantle the stocks or institute their own draconian punishments. A less extreme version of this choice confronts teachers all the time, especially at the secondary level. I have been approached by teachers who feel caught between competing forces *(cont.)*

when implementing changes to their grading methods. Many teachers would like to explore ways to motivate students without the threat of penalties, but fear that their students will then spend the bulk of their time on assignments for classes that do institute penalties. I have chosen the term *interdepartmental cold war* to describe this dilemma.

Of course, because students have a limited amount of time and energy, there will always be some form of competition among teachers. One way to mitigate this would be for all educators to avoid adopting punitive measures that reward compliance rather than evidence of learning.

competency, improvement, and understanding of material.

Strategy #1: Use Incompletes and Interventions Rather Than Zeros

STEP 1: Set due dates and time spans. Due dates for assignments are like the dates we set when inviting friends over for dinner: they serve as promises that are expected to be met. When guests arrive late for dinner, the food gets cold and the visit is often shortened. Broken promises inconvenience others, and a pattern of broken promises can compromise the integrity and credibility of the promise breaker. I let my students know that I work hard to grade them fairly and that I am prepared to invest extra time to that end—not to guilt trip them, but to remind them that I'm keeping up my end of the bargain and expect them to do so as well.

I've had success with setting a time span rather than a due date. Time spans such as "sometime next week" provide students with flexibility and choice. When I give students a week's span to hand in their work, I usually consider Friday to be the true due date, but I am happy to give the impression that there is a range of acceptable dates. Students begin to feel a helpful nudge on Monday as the "early" assignments start trickling in. Whether you've set a due date or time span, it is imperative that students not wait too long to start working on their assignments. A tidal wave of late assignments is unbearable for the teacher, and rushing at the last minute is never in students' best interests.

STEP 2: Use the Late or Incomplete Assignment Form. One day when I was grading papers at home, I noticed that one of my students, Jimmy, hadn't turned in his map assignment. I tried to recall if there was a reason for it to be missing. Was he in class on Friday? Did he tell me he'd hand it in on Monday? Did he misunderstand when it was due? Is he struggling with the content? Was he one of the athletes away on a basketball trip? Sitting at home on a Saturday afternoon, all I could do was speculate.

Luckily, my frustration with not knowing where Jimmy's assignment was led me to design the Late or Incomplete Assignment Form shown in Figure 1.3. Now, when students don't hand in or finish their

Figure 1.3
Late or Incomplete Assignment Form

Name: _____   Date: _____

Missing assignment: _____

Reason(s) for missing the due date:

☐ school-based sports/extracurricular   ☐ heavy course load
☐ job/work requirements   ☐ social event(s)
☐ difficulty with material/lack of understanding   ☐ club or group event out of school
☐ procrastination   ☐ other

Details: _____

_____

_____

Revised completion date: _____

Interventions/support required:

☐ extra study/home-based effort   ☐ use of planner
☐ homework club   ☐ help with time management
☐ extra help from teacher   ☐ counselor visit
☐ tutorial   ☐ other

Details: _____

_____

_____

work, I ask them to fill out the form and explain what happened. The last section of the form asks student to select potential interventions that might help them complete the assignment.

The benefits of this form are twofold. First, the student can actually plan a strategy for completing the assignment. Second, students see what interventions are available in the school to help them: students who are suffering emotionally, for example, might not realize that school counselors are available to talk. This form allows a missing assignment to be the catalyst for students to obtain the support they need to be happy and effective in all classes.

Consider the following example. Greg was a quiet student in my 12th grade history class who had always done fairly well. Suddenly, over the course of a month, he began to accrue absences, he failed to hand in a few assignments, and his quiz and test scores dropped. It is not uncommon for high school seniors to experience a dip in performance, so I did not get too alarmed. Though Greg assured me that he would be able to turn things around, I asked if there were any outside factors affecting his academic life. After a pause and a few too many blinks, he responded.

"I was in a car accident a few weeks back," he said. "That might have something to do with it. I've had a splitting headache ever since."

"A few weeks back!" Further questioning revealed that the accident had occurred about six weeks prior and that he had not sought any medical attention afterward. Rather than focusing on absences, missed assignments, and poor test scores, I worked on connecting Greg with a doctor, a physiotherapist, and a chiropractor. Within about a week, Greg appeared happier and more energetic and reported that his headaches had disappeared. He was soon caught up on his work and doing better than he ever had before.

Teachers should read and sign the Late or Incomplete Assignment Form after students have filled it in. This ensures that teachers hold the students accountable for revised due dates and that they are aware of any issues needing immediate attention. If a student suggests an unreasonably distant completion date, the teacher should feel free to say no and impose a more reasonable time frame. And if a student indicates that his or her underlying issue is particularly grave—neighborhood violence, for example—the teacher should strive to put supports in place for that student as soon as possible.

STEP 3: Implement intervention strategies. Any interventions noted on the Late or Incomplete Assignment Form need to be implemented in a timely manner. If the student suggests that he will turn in the assignment within a day or two, let him prove it; however, if the two days pass and nothing's handed in, it's time to say, "OK, we tried it your way—now it is my turn." Here are some long- and short-term intervention strategies that are worth considering:

- Homework-completion centers that students attend during lunch or after school.
- Saturday school as a requirement for those who are falling behind in their work. The threat of Saturday school is enough to scare many students into completing their assignments.
- In-school suspensions during which students can get support from teachers.
- Pair-ups of older students needing community hours with younger students needing help.

STEP 4: When necessary, assign incompletes. Listing assignments as "incomplete" is preferable than resorting to the finality of the powerful zero. Without a numerical value, an incomplete assignment will not risk dropping a student's final average precipitously for reasons unrelated to the student's understanding of content.

Once a student is afforded the opportunity to complete an assignment, the assignment should be listed as "incomplete" in the grade book until it is completed. In fact, the student's *entire course standing* should be listed as incomplete as long as the assignment isn't finished and handed in. Although some schools or districts may not allow courses to be listed as incomplete on report cards, policies can be challenged and changed. I worked at one school that allowed incompletes on report cards but required that they be converted into numerical values after two weeks. (Often it took a lot less than two weeks to resolve the incompletes—especially after they came to parents' attention.)

If a numerical value is required, it is up to you as the teacher to consider all variables and deliver a final grade that you believe is the best reflection of the student's evidence of learning. Here are some variables to consider when formulating a final numerical grade:

- Conversations with the student
- Quiz scores
- Partial completion of assignments
- Test score patterns
- Attendance

Informed decisions sometimes have to be rendered without every piece of hard evidence in place. The bottom line is that you should do what professionals from oncologists to mechanics to accountants do: examine all the data available and render as accurate an opinion as possible based on your analysis.

Here are some reasons why following the above steps can reap benefits in the classroom:

1. Students have to work hard to achieve zero. When I began instituting time spans for assignments, using the Late or Incomplete Assignment Form, implementing interventions, and assigning incompletes rather than zeros, more students began completing their assignments in my classes than ever before. The change was particularly evident among students who had previously tended to opt out of assignments that they considered to be inconvenient.

I started telling my students on the first day of class, "You'll have to work hard to achieve a zero." I let them know that I considered responsibility, accountability, and—most of all—learning paramount in my class. I told them that if they considered opting out of assignments, they could expect to visit homework-completion centers or Saturday school, and that their lives would be made more difficult by phone calls to their parents and, eventually, an "incomplete" on their report cards. Having sufficiently stunned my students, I ended my rant by reminded them that life would be much easier if they just completed the handful of mandatory graded assignments.

Despite my clear warnings to students, instituting my no-zeros system was not without its struggles and difficult conversations. (See the sidebar on this page for an account of one of them.)

2. The system results in accurate grades. Once students are actually required to complete assignments so that the grades attached to them are real measures of learning, it is easy for teachers to defend the students' grades, which typically improve when zeros and lates are taken out of the equation. This is especially true for average and struggling learners—those in the 60–70 percent range who might be tempted to factor in a few zeros when it's convenient, for example, find that they quickly shoot up to the 80–90 percent range once they're prohibited from opting out of assignments. In addition, students with disruptive home lives no longer face the "double jeopardy" of a dysfunctional environment outside of school added to punitive grades within it.

3. Student results improve. When educators get rid of zeros and lates at a schoolwide level, the results can be incredible. Schools that adopt meaningful consequences rather than resorting to zeros experience lower dropout rates and higher

PERSONAL STORY

One of the most popular activities in my 12th grade history class was our annual re-creation of the 1919 Paris Peace Conference. After students spent a few days conducting careful and focused research on the events leading up to the conference, the school library was transformed into the Palace of Versailles and the students into diplomats attempting to reconfigure post–World War I Europe. Just as in the historical version, our conference always had plenty of arguments, secret deals, and disappointments.

When the conference was over, each student had to write an essay analyzing the conference from the point of view of the country he or she had been chosen to represent and explaining how the activity had helped him or her to better understand the complexities of international negotiations. Students who took the necessary time to research their assigned nationalities and who had invested energy and enthusiasm into the conference negotiations had no problem writing impassioned reflections.

One year, I had a student, Ellen, who failed to complete her essay. As days turned into a week, she kept putting it off, telling me she'd have it done "soon." I reminded Ellen that as long as the assignment was not handed in, her grade for the course would be listed as incomplete. I suspected that Ellen had come to rely on her network of friends to complete her assignments for her, and the reflective nature of the essay did not conform to her "peer-completion system."

After a few more days, I reminded Ellen that her work was still incomplete and that her report card would reflect that fact. When she still didn't hand in her essay, I entered "incomplete" in her report card for the class. *(cont.)*

PERSONAL STORY CONTINUED

The day after report cards had been sent home, Ellen was waiting by my door when I got to class. She was fuming.

"I got my report card and I don't have a grade," she said. "This does not make any sense! Where's my grade?"

"You don't have a numerical score right now," I replied. "Perhaps you'll recall that as long as I don't have your reflection essay, I can't issue you a numerical grade."

"That's stupid," she said. "I should have a grade. My dad saw my report card and he also thinks this is a stupid system."

Though I began to feel defensive, I tried to remain measured. "Perhaps your dad would like to give me a call," I said.

Though I was indeed offended by Ellen's language, I reminded myself that I wasn't the only one experiencing a paradigm shift. *(cont.)*

rates of school completion (Reeves, 2006b; Reeves, 2010). Data from one high school I used to work at support these findings. In 2005, we implemented lunchtime and after-school homework and assignment supports, followed shortly by a Saturday school program. As a result, teachers began to explore consequences for missing assignments that focused on completion rather than punishment. The table in Figure 1.4 shows the total number of course failures before, during, and after these interventions were put in place. (The table reflects failures in all high school courses at a high school with approximately 700 students, meaning that a single student could account for as many of 8 failures in any given year.)

4. Responsibility and accountability are increased. As educators, we do society a great disservice if we do not teach students that behaviors

Figure 1.4
Number of Course Failures Before, During, and After Implementation of "No Zeros" Policy and Additional Supports

Year	Term 1	Term 2	Term 3	Term 4	Final
2004–2005	292	334	321	300	192
2005–2006	215	272	265	291	118
2006–2007	160	198	193	248	104
2007–2008	5	33	40	53	36

Data compiled by Terry Grady.

have consequences. As long as I have students asking me to give them zeros, I will be convinced that zeros do not encourage responsibility but rather erode it.

5. Interventions can be personalized and equitable. Because every student's needs are unique, schools should deliver personalized learning opportunities and interventions (Cooper, 2011; Rshaid, 2011). Some students will require assistance from either a teacher or an older, academically successful student; other students simply need a quiet, structured environment in which to complete assignments. In a personalized learning environment, not every solution matches every student. Once zeros and lates are off the table, educators are empowered to do what is necessary for each student to learn.

Strategy #2: Institute Two-Tiered Testing

It is common for student attendance to dip on test days. Some students simply decide to avoid the discomfort of taking the test. If they have chosen not to prepare for it, they may feel that failure is inevitable.

When I made the shift to basing student grades solely on learning outcomes, I was forced to look for alternatives to grading penalties for students who missed a test. It seemed ludicrous to go to the effort to have students complete all of their assignments in order to grade them accurately, only to turn around and reduce test scores due to truancy. My solution? *Design two different tests*—one for the scheduled test day, and a less user-friendly one for the make-up

A flicker of clarity passed over Ellen's eyes. "I don't have a time."

"That's right," I said. "You don't have a time until you complete all three stages of the triathlon—just as you don't have a final grade until all of your assignments are in."

Ellen then asked a question that drove home to me just how much zeros diminish personal responsibility, sabotage learning, and destroy students' standings: "Can I please just have a zero?"

Her question thudded against my eardrums and reverberated through the room. A student had just *asked* for a zero, and even used the word "please"! For years I had used zeros as the ultimate weapon of persuasion; zero was the hero combating the evil powers of avoidance and apathy and upholding the values of responsibility and accountability. In one fell swoop, Ellen sapped our hero of all its power.

I declined Ellen's request, and she slammed the door as she left the room. A day or two after our heated conversation, Ellen submitted a thoughtful and complete reflection essay. I asked her why she had done such a good job on the essay given that she was so eager for a zero. Her response offered a peek into an adolescent's view of effort and accountability.

"If I'm going to put my name on something, I'm going to do a good job," she said, "even if I didn't want to do it in the first place."

Since my confrontation with Ellen, I have lost count of the number of times students have asked for zeros in place of actually completing their work. Students have offered to clean the classroom, buy me lunch, and wash my car if I would reconsider, just this once, bending my "no zeros" policy. Now, when I hear teachers preach about the need to use zeros to enforce student responsibility and accountability, behind my desire to smirk is the story of Ellen.

test. This is not about making one test that's easy and another one that's hard, but rather an attempt to grant more favorable conditions to students who take the test according to schedule. For example, the more user-friendly test given out on the scheduled test day might allow the student to choose between a number of written response topics.

Another option is to deliver the same test differently on the scheduled test day than on the day of the make-up test. For example, let's say a unit plan has eight reasoning targets that students are supposed to meet. On the scheduled test day, I might place scraps of paper with the numbers one through eight in a hat, select three scraps at random, and let the students pick one of the three selected targets to answer on the test. On the day of the make-up test, I might select only one number, so that the students aren't given a choice. This strategy has the side benefit of removing any bias I might have regarding the targets from the equation.

On the scheduled test day, it can also be fun if you involve the students by having them pick the numbers out of the hat—students enjoy the lottery aspect, and giving the students a choice of targets helps to reduce their stress. The availability of choice also contributes to student confidence: students who might otherwise skip a test on the scheduled day might end up attending if they know that they'll be granted greater leeway than on the make-up test.

If you choose to implement a two-tiered testing system, be clear to students that those taking the test on schedule will be granted more favorable conditions, but that all students will still have a chance to prove their mastery. This two-tiered testing system has the following benefits:

- It sends a message to students that it is in their best interests to complete the test on the scheduled test day.
- Students who take the make-up test still receive grades based entirely on evidence of learning.
- The teacher doesn't have to spend time assessing the legitimacy of each student's absence.
- It is harder for students taking the make-up test to cheat by talking to classmates who took the test on schedule because the formats of the two tests will differ.
- Students who get more time to study by taking the test later receive a slightly more challenging test format, which is only fair.

Students have a keen eye for equity and fairness. Most of them welcome a system that separates behavior-based penalties from the grading process. Students know that some people miss tests for valid reasons and others have circumstances that are murky. Two-tiered testing aligns with the imperatives suggested by Damien Cooper in his book *Redefining Fair* (2011): it's informative, it blends consistency with professional judgment, and it is transparent in both purpose and communication. Perhaps this is why I have not had a single student complaint about or parental challenge to this policy. In fact, one parent specifically told me that she welcomed this system because it stopped her daughter from lobbying her to call the school with an excuse for her absences on scheduled test days.

Strategy #3: Match Consequences to Behaviors

Students, being human, make poor decisions from time to time. As Oscar Wilde once wrote, "Experience is simply the name we give our mistakes." Unfortunately, many educators have fallen into the trap of believing that punitive grading should be the chief consequence for poor decisions and negative behaviors. These teachers continue to argue that grading as punishment works, despite over 100 years of overwhelming research that suggests it does not (Guskey, 2011; Reeves, 2010). Just because a student does her homework doesn't mean that she did so to avoid a grading penalty. As Guskey's (2011) extensive research shows, students do not perform better when they know that "it counts."

Once you decide not to let negative behaviors excessively affect your academic data, the door is wide open to explore the use of consequences that are unique, purposeful, and effective. It's impossible to design a universal rulebook that addresses every potential student infraction; in fact, overreliance on one-size-fits-all penalties reflects precisely the mentality that most limits teachers from making professional decisions for individual students. Once rules are set in stone, educators are painted into a corner. Administrators will be quick to agree that teachers are most often the ones asking that certain rules *not* be applied in particular cases. The fact is that most teachers do not want students to be expelled or to fail a course due to poor decision making or challenging circumstances. Rather, we want guidelines in place that encourage positive choices and compel students to do what's necessary for them to succeed academically.

Schools can develop guidelines for confronting negative behaviors such as truancy, defiance, tardiness, plagiarism, and a host of others that extend far beyond the realm of grading. Such guidelines can help teachers to modify their approach based on the issues affecting each individual student. The following examples from my own experience show a few ways in which negative behaviors can be curbed without reducing student grades.

Example 1: Student Plagiarizes Speech

Background: During the last two weeks of a senior leadership class, each student was asked to deliver a speech describing "what leadership means to me." An otherwise academically successful student, Gina, delivered a speech that was found to have been heavily plagiarized. Prior to the infraction, Gina's grade in the class stood at 97 percent.

Traditional Response: The speech is given a zero, reducing Gina's grade in the class to 94 percent.

Problems with the Traditional Response:

- Gina is content with a grade of 94 percent and readily accepts the consequence.
- The teacher is frustrated by Gina's apparent apathy.
- Gina's revised grade no longer reflects her actual level of academic competency.
- Gina avoids completing an assignment that all the other students completed.

Alternative Response: Gina is required to complete a second speech under the supervision of an adult in an established homework-completion room during her free time (e.g., at lunchtime or after school). In her new speech, Gina is required to discuss her decision to plagiarize the first speech. In addition, she is required to conduct research on the consequences for plagiarism meted out at three different colleges, one of which is the school she is most likely to attend. The teacher informs her parents of Gina's plagiarism and of the resulting consequences. Her second speech is graded as normal, with no penalties applied.

Benefits of the Alternative Response:

- The behavioral infraction (plagiarizing to save time and effort) is met with a behavioral consequence (losing free time and having to expend additional effort).
- Because Gina cares about losing her free time, she takes the consequence seriously.
- A teachable moment is realized as Gina learns about the consequences she can expect if she plagiarizes in college
- Gina's grade in the class is preserved as reflective entirely of her knowledge of prescribed learning outcomes.

Example 2: Student Delivers Project Three Days Late

Background: During a unit on ancient Egypt, all 5th grade students are asked to complete a poster on four different aspects of Egyptian society. One student, Simon, wastes time in class rather than work on his poster, so the teacher asks him to complete the assignment at home. The next day, Simon still hasn't finished it. Three days later, he hands in the completed poster.

Traditional Response: The teacher applies a penalty of 10 percent off per day late. The poster would have received a score of 62 percent if handed in on time, but because it is three days late, the grade is reduced to 32 percent. The teacher hears Simon mutter, "Next time I won't even bother getting it done." Simon's overall class grade drops from 58 percent to 49 percent.

Problems with the Traditional Response:

- The score of 32 percent does not reflect the actual quality of the poster or Simon's level of academic ability.
- Simon's overall grade in the class no longer accurately reflects his academic ability.
- Simon, who would have been on the edge of academic success, now regrets having spent time and effort on the assignment.

Alternative Response: When the teacher notices Simon wasting time in class, she reminds him that he may have to complete the poster at lunchtime or after school. She also tells the class that lates and zeros are not options for those who procrastinate, and encourages students to ask her for help and to let her know if challenges outside the classroom might prevent them from completing the assignment by the next day.

When Simon fails to submit the poster assignment after a day or two, the teacher directs him to an established homework-completion room, where he completes the poster during lunchtime sessions. His final grade on the poster does not reflect any academic penalty.

Benefits of the Alternative Response:

- The response reflects a supportive classroom environment where grading is based strictly according to learning outcomes.
- The behavioral infraction (wasting time in class) is met with a behavioral consequence (missing free time at lunch). Because Simon can see the connection between wasting class time and losing free time, he is liable to be more accountable in the future.
- Simon is encouraged by his penalty-free grade and realizes the connection between effort and reward.

Example 3: Student Delivers Perfect Project Two Days Late and Parent Lobbies for No Grading Penalty

Background: During an 8th grade science unit on planets, Serena delivers an exceptional clay project displaying the size and color of the planets. Unfortunately, she hands in her project two days late, along with a note from her mother highlighting some medical concerns in the family that contributed to the tardiness and requesting that the teacher call her so she can explain the details. Serena's teacher is concerned, as he knows her to be not only a perfectionist, but also generally punctual. He recalls that a similar situation arose with one of her projects a month earlier. Despite the note from Serena's mother, the teacher feels that it would not be fair to the other students if he were to give her a high score on the project. As he sees it, Serena appears to have benefitted from extra time to complete it.

Traditional Response: The teacher applies a penalty to Serena's project of 10 percent off per day late, leading to an increasingly uncomfortable series of phone calls with Serena's irate mother and, eventually, the principal's involvement. In the end, the teacher is forced to rescind the late penalty and give Serena a perfect score. Around the time that the situation is resolved, another project is due that Serena will once again not hand in on time.

Problems with the Traditional Response:

- Serena's mother appears to be enabling her poor choices.
- Serena is learning that the system can be altered to suit her needs.
- Serena may eventually encounter a system, perhaps at the post-secondary level, that will not bend to the wishes of her mother.
- An unfair playing field has been established in which Serena can take extra time to complete an assignment as long as a parent can lobby to eliminate the penalty. Other parents and students are unhappy about this development.

Alternative Response: The teacher decides that regardless of the circumstances, each student's work will be graded solely on the basis of learning outcomes and uses the Late or Incomplete Assignment Form to track the reasons for handing in assignments after they're due. If a student's forms suggest a predictable pattern of late assignments, the teacher can thereafter assign that student to homework-completion sessions either before or after the assignment is due. If a student misses assignments for reasons that require further explanation, the teacher simply offers support, perhaps by meeting with the student at lunch or after school to fill out the form and discuss the situation.

Benefits of the Alternative Response:

- The teacher only grades the assignments according to learning outcomes.
- All students who need academic or behavioral support receive it, thus increasing their accountability.
- The effect of negative parental influences on grades is eliminated.

Example 4: Students Misuse Cell Phones in Class

Background: Cell phone use has hit epidemic levels in Mr. Sanchez's carpentry class. The students' inattentiveness to their teacher's demonstrations and to their surroundings presents both academic and safety hazards. Mr. Sanchez argues for implementing a strict no-phones policy at staff meetings, but his fellow teachers object because some of their lessons actually incorporate the students' cell phones. Frustrated, Mr. Sanchez decides to apply a grading penalty whenever student are caught using phones in his class.

Traditional Response: Mr. Sanchez introduces a daily classroom behavior grade ranging from zero to five, and students caught texting receive automatic zeros for the day. By the end of the term, some students' overall scores are diminished considerably due to their phone use. Mr. Sanchez also decides to confiscate the cell phones of chronic offenders.

Problems with the Traditional Response:

- Students' behavioral decisions result in grades that do not reflect their learning.
- Mr. Sanchez is forced to consider a behavior grade for every student every day, resulting in much more work for him as well as pressure to watch all students closely at all times.
- Some students may gladly "pay" in daily behavior grades in order to continue texting in class.
- Students whose phones are confiscated can become angry and conflict can ensue.

Alternative Response: An administrator visits every class in the school and explains the introduction of an initiative designed to help students make wise choices about cell phone use. In addition, teachers are given the freedom to establish phone-use norms specific to their classes. Students are encouraged to ask their teachers if they may use their phones in the event that personal circumstances require them to call or text during class. Administrators inform everyone in the school community that teachers will direct students to the main office for recurring infractions. In such cases, students' phones can be confiscated for the day and held until their parents retrieve them. There is no grading penalty for classroom cell phone use.

Benefits of the Alternative Response:

- The behavioral infraction (cell phone use) is met with a suitable behavioral consequence (cell phone confiscation).
- Teachers can focus on delivering instruction rather than constantly monitoring phone use.
- Administrators are given the opportunity to examine why students are using their phones in class and seek applicable interventions.
- Parents are informed of and involved in the process.
- Individual teachers are free to incorporate student cell phone use in lesson plans.

Frequently Asked Questions

Q: If I don't apply grades, students won't do the work—it's that simple. What do you suggest I do instead?

A: I think we need to question the validity of the idea that things won't get done unless they're graded. Consider the following points:

- "Getting it done" does not mean that learning occurred.
- Many factors other than grades can compel students to submit assignments.
- Faced with grading penalties, many students will still fail to do the work required.
- Grading penalties aimed at completion compel some students to cheat.
- Forcing students to complete assignments on time will inevitably come at the expense of something else.
- Educators risk sending the message that they will alter the intended purpose of grading—measuring learning outcomes— to affect student behavior.

Educators who need proof that grading penalties do not lead to increased effort or more learning are encouraged to study the work of Tom Guskey (2011). The bottom line is that when activities are engaging, purposeful, and personal, students will be interested regardless of the grading consequences.

Q: Aren't grading penalties the logical consequences of poor student choices?

A: I once had a conversation with a teacher who was adamant that grading penalties were justifiable as the logical consequences of students' poor choices. Here is my recollection of our conversation:

Janet: I have to give Jimmy a zero. I'm sorry, but if something is not handed in and the learning outcomes were not demonstrated, then it's a zero.

Me: Regardless of what you think he may or may not have learned?

Janet: Listen, I'm not going to guess. Furthermore, I've chased Jimmy around. Sorry, but I am done.

Me: So you're making a punitive decision?

Janet: I guess so, but it's the logical consequence. Show up late to a job, and you're fired!

Me: I know a number of people who show up late for work fairly regularly and are still employed—but let's discuss grading for the moment. I hate applying zeros as a penalty because it renders the rest of my grading useless.

Janet: Zero is not a penalty if it reflects something that wasn't done at all! Jimmy did no work, so there is no grade—that isn't some arbitrary decision. I don't get why you keep saying that zero is a penalty; it's simply an accurate reflection of the fact that nothing was done.

Me: Except that you're choosing a number that is far from the likeliest outcome had the student done the work. For nearly every student, 100 percent would be more likely than zero. Wouldn't you agree?

Janet: I guess so, but I want to teach the students a lesson as well.

Me: Have you ever been on a school committee that requires you to collect money from fellow staff members?

Janet: Yeah, why?

Me: Did teachers bring in their money when asked to?

Janet: No, it is impossible to collect money from some teachers!

Me: I haven't collected money, but I've collected award-nomination sheets from teachers. The barrier wasn't high: I asked teachers to put their names on a sheet and fill it in to whatever extent they wished. They could even leave it blank if they wanted. Despite two weeks of reminders and even a few warnings, many of the teachers failed to hand in their sheets. In fact, on the day of the awards ceremony, long after the trophies were engraved, I had teachers ask if I could possibly accept their nominations. I find it interesting that many of these same teachers won't accept assignments from struggling learners a single day late without applying a penalty.

When will we accept that procrastination is a human condition? Just because certain teachers didn't hand in nomination sheets doesn't mean that they didn't have students who deserved an award—and just because a student procrastinates doesn't mean that he doesn't know, say, the causes of World War II. Evidence of understanding is not dependent on a due date.

Janet: But what about that one kid who pushes it—the one who ignores all my efforts? That 1 percent of the population?

Me: I don't write policy for all my students based on the one student in my class who falls outside the norm. I prefer to use professional discretion.

Q: You said that you post incompletes instead of student grades if essential assignments aren't completed. What do you do if a numerical course standing is required?

A: The following example provides a few potential solutions to this dilemma. Vince was a senior in high school who seemed to enjoy my history class, attending regularly and taking part in class conversations. His favorite course in school was theater, and he was a regular cast member in our school's drama productions. When he did miss history class, it was usually due to obligations related to major drama productions.

The last unit of the year in history class was on the Cold War. On the day of the last unit test, Vince was absent. I was surprised, as this was the first time he'd missed a test day. It turned out that Vince had left the community entirely: a student who knew him told me that he was attending an audition for an acting school.

With only a week left in the school year, I knew that I faced a difficult decision. I gave Vince an "incomplete" on his unit test, which in turn made his overall class grade "incomplete" as well. It had become my mission to only grade on hard evidence, and I was frustrated at the prospect that I might have to alter my system due to Vince's departure. I considered assessing his knowledge of the Cold War by phone, but I couldn't get in touch with him.

The last day of the school year arrived and I still did not have a score for Vince's unit test. When the school secretary asked what grade should be reported for Vince, I didn't know what to say. She informed me that the British Columbia Ministry of Education would not accept "incomplete" as a grade. I was given one hour to decide on a numerical grade. Here are the variables I considered:

- Vince had attended all but two classes of the three-week Cold War unit.

I shared the saga of how I decided on Vince's final grade with a group of teachers once. One of the teachers, an experienced educator named Bob, agreed with my position of grading only according to learning outcomes, but felt that I was bending my principles by submitting anything other than a zero for Vince's missing test score.

"You change the math to fit your needs!" he said. "When it doesn't work out, you just pick an arbitrary number. Vince may as well have received a zero—at least that would've reflected the certainty that there was no assessment evidence at all. You resorted to a hunch!"

When Bob mentioned the "hunch," I thought about how valuable hunches are in other situations. I asked Bob, "Imagine that you visit your knee surgeon, and after she looks at your x-rays, she tells you that 95 percent of the time, the condition you have results in a typical surgical procedure. However, given what she knows about your specific case, she's got a hunch that another option just might work. Would you think that her hunch was valid?"

Reluctantly, Bob responded that he probably would. Just as there is great value in a personal opinion based on professional experience, there is also great value in a professional opinion based on personal experience.

- I could recall at least two class discussions in which Vince participated during the unit, his contributions to which certainly reflected a degree of interest in and understanding of the issues.
- Vince had never failed a single test in history class. His scores were fairly consistent across all units, with nearly every test score landing somewhere between 73 and 79 percent.
- Vince had completed a few quizzes on Cold War topics, with an average score of about 70 percent.

Based on these variables, I decided that I had the following options:

1. Enter a zero for the test and report Vince's final grade as 71 percent.
2. Omit the missing test and report the final grade as 76 percent.
3. Use the average of all of Vince's unit-test scores as the final grade. Because his test scores were typically higher than his grades on assignments, the result would be a final grade of 77 percent.
4. Enter a score for the missing test equal to that of his lowest unit-test grade: 75 percent.
5. Enter score for the missing test greater than zero but lower than 73, so that it would be impossible for the score to improve his grade.

In the end, I went with the last option: I entered a score of 35 percent for the missing test, resulting in a final grade of 73 percent.

2

HOMEWORK

Why do you keep asking for my homework?
I never have it done and I don't think I ever will.

—former 12th grade history student

I have visited many schools and districts in North America, and one argument rises above all others whenever it is suggested that we stop grading identical homework assignments. It is a version of the same question we covered in Chapter 1: "I have to grade it or my students will not do it." The conundrum surrounding homework is a global phenomenon, as became clear to me when I was asked to speak at a 2011 conference of the Near East South Asia (NESA) Council of Overseas Schools in Athens, Greece. The educators who attend this conference are from international schools with student populations that consist mainly of foreign nationals and the children of wealthy local families. When I mentioned at the conference that I had stopped grading uniform homework, these educators voiced the same concerns I'd heard in North America, and added that they thought parents would be dismayed if their kids weren't assigned plenty of graded homework.

I understand the dilemma that educators face in cultures and communities where there are entrenched beliefs about homework completion and grading. What I have experienced over the last number of years, however, has caused me to question how *effective* uniform homework is, either for measuring learning or for motivating students to learn.

Before we go on, let's be clear on what I mean by "uniform homework." I'm referring to assignments designed to serve as follow-up or practice for what has already been covered in class. Such assignments are usually designed to yield identical answers from every student. Assigning the homework usually goes something like this: "OK, class, that ends the lesson on multiplying fractions. I showed you how to solve a few examples; now for homework, I want everyone to complete numbers 1–20 on page 88." I am not referring to personalized assignments or projects that are started in class but require more time to complete.

In 2006, I basically stopped grading uniform homework altogether, and I immediately experienced a number of pleasing consequences. For one, my quality of life improved: because I spent far less time grading homework that I often suspected had been completed by someone other than the student, I was able to spend more time with my family and riding my mountain bike on weekends, and I had more time to plan assignments that involved deeper thinking and personal ownership. Additionally, by removing data from my grade book that merely reflected completion and compliance, I saw that the aggregate data began to more accurately reflect student understanding.

Problems with Grading Homework

In order to understand why educators might consider changing their view of uniform homework, it may be valuable to identify a few problems with the traditional approach.

Grading Homework Confuses Completion with Understanding

Educators seem to believe that they are tasked with instilling work ethic into today's youth. I have heard many teachers demand that students do their homework because it is "the right thing to do." Many educators have said to me that if we don't teach our students the value of work before they enter the workforce, society will pay dearly. The problem with this well-intended argument is that attaching a grade to homework inevitably leads to grading completion rather than understanding. Educators have been so thoroughly blending the assessment of completion with the assessment of understanding for so long that it's become impossible for many of them to separate the two components (O'Connor, 2010).

Let's assume that educators the world over believe that a strong work ethic, a sense of responsibility, and a willingness to put forth genuine effort are all fantastic human attributes worthy of promoting in school. Having personally taught in three distinctly different political jurisdictions, and having worked with educators representing hundreds more, I have yet to see these attributes listed as measurable *learning* outcomes by any governing authority. Not only have I never been asked to assign a number grade to these qualities, I wouldn't really know how to do it if I were required to.

To be clear, there is nothing wrong with instilling a good work ethic in students. In his book *Outliers* (2008), Malcolm Gladwell argues rather convincingly that spending 10,000 hours on any given task may just make you both very proficient and very rich. Actions that encourage increased student effort should generally be applauded. The issue is not the value of hard work, but rather the manner in which it is represented.

Grading Homework Promotes Busy Work at the Expense of Intrinsic Motivation and Authentic Learning

It is both unfortunate and ironic that our efforts to instill a good work ethic in our students through graded homework might be achieving exactly the stated goal, just not as we envision it: students may indeed focus on working hard, but at the expense of authentic learning. Educators will note that employees don't get paid if they fail to work hard. Although this is true, the evidence shows that intrinsic motivation decreases once people are paid to do what they used to do for fun (Pink, 2009). Who could argue that intrinsic motivation is not necessary for authentic learning? We should embrace practices that promote investigation and inquiry and jettison those that deter exploration. (You'll find more on the importance of investigation and inquiry in Chapter 5.)

Grading Homework Results in Inflated Grades (and Cheating)

Grades can be either inflated or deflated when teachers decide to assess homework, especially as students may learn that exertion of effort will yield a better grade on a report than actual learning. My colleague Chris Van Bergeyk, principal of Summerland Secondary School in Summerland, British Columbia, put it this way:

> Hard-working students get extra marks through completing homework without deepening their understanding. It's akin to bonus marks—students may be tempted to spend two hours on homework to make it look great, and to subsequently receive the extra 10 percent for completion. Homework really acts as a grading cushion for many students, especially hard-working ones.

Homework that *appears* to be the result of genuine effort may not actually be the result of genuine effort. Some students have become accustomed to bolstering their academic standing by making sure to consistently deliver homework that appears to be of high quality, regardless of its origin. That's right, I am suggesting that some students might be copying the homework of others—there, I said it! My most recent Google search for "cheating on homework" generated 11,600,000 hits—clearly, this is a problem. A study conducted in 2005 indicated that nearly 70 percent of U.S. high school students admitted to cheating on at least one exam during the previous year (Grimes & Rezek, 2005). Another study conducted across nine U.S. colleges revealed that fully 75 percent of the 1,800 students surveyed admitted to cheating on tests and written assignments (Fang & Casadevall, 2013). Students are more likely to cheat if they believe that other students are cheating (Blachnio & Weremko, 2011) and if they fear the loss of something, such as reputation or ranking (Rick & Loewenstein, 2008).

Not all teachers feel that the statistics cited above represent their classrooms. One seasoned Kentucky high school educator who based 50 percent of his students' grades on homework told me unequivocally that his students have *never* cheated. Unfortunately for the rest of us, it is quite likely that many of our students have copied each other's homework. It is tempting for educators to unleash our wrath on students who are caught cheating; we tend to shame them, lambast them, and subject them to the punitive zero.

Catching and identifying students who cheat is not necessarily the best way to combat the problem—after all, despite our best efforts, we probably only catch a small fraction of the cases. As my mom is fond of repeating, "If you catch one mouse, there are still another 10 to be found!" Some teachers grow so weary of fighting the seemingly inevitable issue of cheating that they take to approving of or even recommending that students collaborate with each other on homework. The merits of teamwork and collegiality aside, grades awarded for group efforts are usually recorded for individual students, thereby misrepresenting their level of actual learning (O'Connor, 2010). I can assure you that had I been given the option of collaborating on homework as a student, my physics homework would have more accurately been a measure not of my learning but of the extent to which I had a bright and generous friend who understood the assignment.

In some cases, students may actually believe they are doing their own homework but have become so accustomed to working with others that they don't realize it when someone else has done the bulk of the deeper thinking, problem solving, and processing. Such students may find that their test scores are significantly lower than their homework grades. Ask any group of teachers how their students explain such a discrepancy and they will unanimously answer, "Test anxiety!" This, too, appears to be a global phenomenon: seemingly intelligent, high-functioning students are suddenly afflicted with a condition that blocks their ability to re-create on a test the clear understanding reflected so recently on their high-quality homework. Am I the only one who finds the timing of this destructive and elusive condition very interesting? I am sure that true, clinically proven test anxiety exists, but I also believe that many cases of it would evaporate *if students actually did their own homework.* I can guarantee you that I would have had severe test anxiety if I'd gotten good grades on my physics homework because someone else had done it for me—maybe even enough for me to conveniently pass out.

Some students may be able to work together on homework assignments and rely upon the academic prowess of their peers. Students as young as kindergartners are capable of positively influencing their classmates both academically and behaviorally (Smith & Fowler, 1984). More recent research indicates that a positive peer culture results in better student behavior (Goodwin & Miller, 2012). However, these benefits may not be as accessible to at-risk students—after all, students prone to truancy and other behavioral infractions often find like-minded friends (Cho, Hallfors, & Sanchez, 2005). Expecting students who identify both personally and socially as nonacademic to benefit from well-intentioned plans for collaborative homework will probably result in disappointment.

Of course, clandestine homework completion can come from sources other than students. Just ask any group of teachers if they have ever wondered how many homework assignments were the handiwork of students' parents, and soon the room will be full of raised hands, snickers, and exhausted faces. To dump a little salt in the wound, follow up by asking whether the teachers consider the grades that they assign to such work to be valuable for measuring student learning. There are few better examples of a rhetorical question. Further complicating matters is the fact that what one parent might consider "a little help," another might consider outright cheating. Leveling accusations of cheating at frustrated and desperate parents will invite painful conversations that we'd all rather avoid.

Sometimes teachers suspect that hired tutors have completed much of their students' homework, particularly in communities where academic competition is fierce. Parents may feel compelled to do whatever it takes for their kids to gain an academic upper hand, and the tutors have a vested interest in making sure that students get as good a grade as possible on their work. Questionable tutorial practices aside, consider the amount of the homework-completion assistance that students have access to online: it is now easier than ever for them to acquire answers to homework questions without exhibiting any personal knowledge or skill.

Grading Homework Results in Deflated Grades (and Disillusion)

A colleague of mine, Cindy Postlethwaite, has spent the majority of her teaching career working with at-risk learners. Cindy was a frequent sounding

PERSONAL STORY

A number of years ago, I observed two of my students—let's call them Steven and Brianna—sitting in our high school lunchroom with their binders open to the same page. Brianna was writing feverishly in hers while Steven sat calmly. Brianna would pause every now and then to look over at Steven's work, then resume writing on her paper. Anyone who has even the slightest familiarity with student behavior would recognize this as classic copying behavior.

After watching quietly for a short while, I could see that the material Brianna was copying was not from my course. I approached the two students and asked what they were doing.

"We're just finishing up some homework," replied Brianna.

Steven hesitated for a moment, casting glances at both Brianna and me. He then added, "Yeah—we are completing our homework."

"How often do you copy homework like this?" I asked.

"I know it's not the right thing to do," replied Brianna, not really answering my question.

"Really, I'm curious: how often do you do this?"

"Mr. Dueck," said Brianna, "I worked late last night, and this homework is worth 10 percent of my grade, and I—"

Steven interrupted: "About half the time." Brianna gave Steven a cold stare, but he was unperturbed. "Hey, it's April and I'm in 12th grade, so I don't have much time left here. Do you really want to know how it works?"

"I would love to know," I responded.

"You're not going to actually tell him, are you, Steven?" Brianna said. *(cont.)*

board for me when I first started down the path to overturning some of my most entrenched grading rules. The research literature suggests that struggling learners can expect to see the greatest academic gains when their teachers adopt nontraditional grading methods (Black & Wiliam, 1998). This is especially true for homework. Cindy used the term *double jeopardy* to describe situations in which struggling learners who already face many obstacles to success in the classroom are hit yet again by punitive homework grades. The incomplete homework of at-risk learners is probably more reflective of the sparse support such students tend to have outside of school than anything else—a notion backed up by recent brain research that points to a correlation between the emotional state of students' home lives and their ability to succeed in school (Medina, 2008). For many students, home might be the worst environment imaginable in which to grapple with challenging academic material. Even when parents sincerely wish to help their kids with homework, they often don't have the necessary skills and knowledge to help; as they struggle and sometimes fight over the seemingly insurmountable assignment on the kitchen table before them, the academic penalty awaiting the student the next morning must cast a rather dismal shadow.

Grading Homework Perpetuates Extrinsic Dependency

Teachers have helped to train generations of students to expect that *everything* they do in class or in preparing for a course should result in some kind of grade. Many teachers grade each quiz, every piece of homework, all class presentations, and anything that remotely resembles a project. I certainly graded a lot of things, and I don't think I was alone. In light of this overzealous propensity to grab a red pen at any opportunity, we should not be overly surprised if students initially respond to ungraded work with apathy: *if there is no grade, why bother doing it?* After all, students are conditioned to expect grades for work that matters. A friend and colleague of mine, Scott Harkness, explains how he successfully weaned his 12th grade biology students away from such conditioning:

> I used to give students marks for completing homework. I dangled marks in front of them like a carrot in front of a horse and carriage. I thought I could use marks to motivate their behavior, but the problem was that the students who cared about the marks were not the ones I needed to worry about. Students who had more spare time, more motivation, or more support at home were getting great homework marks. Those who didn't have those benefits were losing ever more ground. As a result, one semester, I made the switch: homework is no longer represented in the grade book.
>
> The big question was, "How can I get them to complete homework if I don't give them a reward or punishment?" After a lot of thought and collaboration with other educators, I realized that it is all about the buy-in. If students see that the homework is worthwhile, they will put the time in to finish it. If it seems trivial, they won't.

PERSONAL STORY

Cindy and I worked together with the same student—let's call him Jon—throughout his high school years. I worked with him in a social studies class for students identified as being at risk for failure, and Cindy worked with him in the school's learning assistance area. In middle school, Jon had struggled both academically and behaviorally. By the 9th grade, his issues had become so severe that he was at risk of being removed from the school district altogether. However, over the 10th and 11th grades, Jon's academic standing improved tremendously as his negative behaviors receded. Though we suspected that his improvement was due to a host of variables, we were drawn to one in particular: Jon had experienced systemic changes in our school's grading policy. One of the changes that I adopted for Jon and the rest of my class was the elimination of graded homework. In fact, I virtually eliminated homework.

Shortly before Jon graduated, we asked if he and his mom would be willing to share their story. We set up a video camera in our library one day after school, and over the course of a few hours they talked about the challenges Jon had faced and the success he had in overcoming them. When the conversation shifted to the topic of homework, Jon's mom became quite animated. Here are some of her quotes from that segment of the video:

"As we progressed into the 5th, 6th, and 7th grades, things were getting worse and worse. The homework was just unbearable. I mean the crying, the whining, the screaming, the bawling—and that's just me, not even him! . . .

"And it just got worse—he didn't want to do the homework. If a kid is sitting at the table with his eyes closed, how do you   *(cont.)*

Working under the flipped-classroom
model, my students' homework is to watch video
notes so they come to class ready to develop
understanding of those concepts through
discussion groups, activities, and labs. At first,
some students didn't do the homework. I would
touch base with each one and find out the
reason. Did they have hockey, dance, or work all
night? Were they sick? Did they forget? Whatever
the reason, I would record it. If it happened once
in a while, I wouldn't say a thing. If it became a
trend, we would have a longer discussion.

Now, if the students don't finish their
homework, they have to do it first before they can
participate in the discussion group, activity, or
lab. I make sure that the activities following the
video homework assignments are engaging and
interesting. Students are pretty quick to notice that
these are something that they want to be a part of.

Grading Homework Perpetuates the Disadvantages Faced by Lower-Income Students

Eric Jensen's 2009 book *Teaching with Poverty
in Mind* is a groundbreaking work that every public
educator should read. In its first three chapters
alone, Jensen shares with the reader the many challenges faced by students living with poverty. It is
hard to find elements of poverty that don't affect
students' abilities to effectively complete homework
assignments. According to Jensen, students living
with poverty

- Are more likely to live in a crowded home.
- Inherit low self-esteem.
- Own fewer books and watch more TV than their peers.
- Inherit negative views of school.
- Have a 50 percent chance of dealing with evictions, utility disconnections, overcrowding, or lack of a refrigerator.
- Have mentally adapted to suboptimal conditions.
- Are tardy and absent more often than their peers.
- Have more physical altercations more often than their peers.
- Are more likely than their peers to experience physical punishment.

One educator, Michelle Nikisch of Washington State, wrote to me describing the searing reality of utility disconnection for one of her students:

> I just wanted to share that I stopped grading homework the day I found out that one of my students had to wait until her father came home from work so that she could stand out in the gravel driveway and use the headlights from his truck to complete her homework. It was not fair of me to ask a student to do that. That day, I realized I could never again ask a student to stand outside in the elements just for a homework grade.

For students living under these conditions, grading penalties for incomplete homework are yet one more negative consequence of poverty. Perhaps our grading policies should be written more explicitly: "Any homework assignments that fail to be completed due to violence in the home, eviction, sexual exploitation, mental health issues, depression, or utility disconnection will result in a zero." We as educators can never be certain of the reasons that homework is incomplete, so perhaps we should stop assuming that it's always due to lack of effort. A safer and more equitable assumption to make is that all of our students, and especially those facing poverty issues, may have challenges in their lives that render homework completion difficult or impossible. To assign academic penalties for infractions beyond students' control is academically inaccurate and morally wrong.

Making Homework Meaningful

Thankfully, strategies exist for making homework more meaningful and linked much more closely to student achievement than is the case when assignments are simply assigned grades.

Strategy #1: In-Class Quizzes

This strategy involves developing a set of quizzes based on homework assignments. For example, a teacher might assign students a practice sheet of 20 questions in support of an in-class math lesson, then *suggest* that they work on the questions at home *to further their understanding*. To facilitate students' self-assessments, the teacher might provide the correct answers either on an answer sheet or online. (A teacher using the flipped-classroom model might provide the entire lesson online for students to watch as often as they'd like.) The teacher would *not* ask students to submit the practice sheet, and therefore it would not be graded. Next, the teacher could give students a very short in-class quiz to assess a *sampling* of the type of understanding that homework would otherwise enforce. In this case, the teacher might give students a worksheet featuring, say, 20 fraction problems, and *recommend* that they complete as many as possible; the next day, the teacher could administer a quiz consisting of five similar questions. The teacher could then render the scores on the quiz summative by inputting them into a grading program, or preferably elect to make them formative by adjusting the grading program according to both individual and class results. If the grades are recorded as summative, I would strongly recommend adding a make-up quiz for any students who want to demonstrate their improved understanding.

This strategy is effective for the following reasons:

1. When compared to uniform homework, an in-class quiz is a much more accurate representation of each student's ability and understanding. There is little doubt that each in-class quiz is completed by the student whose name adorns the page. Students quickly recognize that the landscape has shifted to a measure of individual responsibility rather than a nebulous concoction of completion indicators. Those who truly benefit from collaborative work are free to join as many homework groups as they wish, but will experience a nasty jolt on their quiz results if they lean on hard-working friends for too long. Parents who demand that their children receive more graded homework should come to value this system; the only parents who may not like the change are those who enjoy getting good grades themselves on what are ostensibly their kids' homework assignments.

2. Because the in-class quiz is completed in a controlled, quiet, and safe environment, it is fairer and more equitable than conventional homework. Students who must work after school or who live in emotionally unstable homes shouldn't be penalized for factors outside of their control. Although such students may have less time to study for a quiz, the quiz, unlike homework, isn't measuring the amount of time each student had in a secure environment the night before, but rather the extent to which each student understands the learning objectives. Teachers I have spoken with who have switched to using in-class quizzes rather than uniform homework report feeling much better about the heightened sense of fairness in their classrooms.

3. Because there are fewer questions to grade in in-class quizzes than in traditional homework, teachers face less work and students receive feedback faster. Research indicates that providing students with feedback as soon as possible increases their interest in the learning process (Rice & Bunz, 2006). This is another example of grading smarter rather than harder. Clearly, it benefits both students and teachers to save time and devote more energy to diversifying learning in the classroom. My friend and colleague Ben Arcuri teaches 12th grade chemistry. In his early teaching experience, he regularly assigned students 15- to 20-question worksheets to be completed at home, which he then graded. Here's how he describes the benefits that accrued when he switched to using in-class quizzes instead:

> I feel I have greatly improved the efficiency and effectiveness of my homework system. Students now only complete homework questions that relate to the concepts they did not understand from the lesson or the questions they got wrong on the in-class quiz. A variety of practice questions and answers can be found in the textbook or on my website, so I no longer photocopy reams of handouts. The students can check their own answers whenever they wish. My students have taken more personal ownership and control over their learning. I no longer assign, collect, mark, re-mark, or record worksheets and homework. Consequently, homework is all practice and no longer forms any part of students' summative grades. Compact quizzes designed around specific learning outcomes are administered during my class and can quickly indicate each student's level of understanding in a much more efficient and effective way. The results are immediate and I can direct help to those who need it most.

Students in Ben's class can track their own progress on quizzes, and because the quizzes are linked to specific learning targets, they can customize their homework tasks to reflect what they most need to study. The forms in Figures 2.1 and 2.2 allow students to use homework questions for effective practice—and more importantly, to take ownership of their own learning processes.

4. Frequent quizzes lead to increased learning. According to a recent study by Kent State University, frequent testing that involves recall of information from memory improves learning. Katherine Rawson (2010) notes that "practice tests—particularly ones

Figure 2.1
Homework Planning Form

Name: _____ Class: _____

Section	Prescribed Learning Outcome	Topic	Homework Support *List all homework that will assist you in understanding the topic.*	Check Off If Complete
2.1	D1–D5	Dynamic Equilibrium		
2.2	D4, D6	Characteristics of Equilibrium		
2.3	D7–D9	Spontaneous or Non-spontaneous	Worksheet 2-1	
2.4	E1–E4	LCP (LeChatelier's Principle)		
2.5	E5	Haber Process	Worksheet 2-2	
2.6	F1–F3	Keq		
2.7	F4	LCP and Keq		
2.8	F5–F8	ICE tables	Worksheet 2-3	

Figure 2.2
Assessment Tracking Sheet

Name: _____ Class: _____

Use this form to keep track of your scores on quizzes and unit tests. Be sure to note the specific concepts that you need to review following a quiz or test.

Quiz/Test	Score	Concepts to Review
Sec 2.1–2.3		
Re-Quiz Sec 2.1–2.3		
Sec 2.4–2.5		
Re-Quiz Sec 2.4–2.5		
Sec 2.6–2.8		
Re-Quiz Sec 2.6–2.8		
Chapter 2 Test		
Chapter 2 Retest		

that involve attempting to recall something from memory—can drastically increase the likelihood that you'll be able to remember that information again later."

5. Homework can be used as a formative assessment tool. Educators who wish to use homework-completion data to figure out the next steps without affecting students' grades can take comfort in doing so. This can be a huge relief to educators. Ideally, homework gives students a chance to practice and to explore, to make errors and figure things out. Once students learn to assess their own homework using answer keys or information from teachers' websites, they can better prepare for their graded assessments.

Strategy #2: Creating Homework Profiles

A few years ago, while visiting a school near Houston, Texas, I shared with the staff that I had stopped grading uniform homework. After showing them some examples of classroom lessons that I had brought with me, a few frustrated members of the math department took issue with the fact that all of them were from humanities courses. As one educator put it, "Your students can memorize the reasons Hitler came to power, but our students need homework practice in order to entrench an understanding of mathematical principles."

I acknowledged that our courses were indeed different, particularly in terms of how much practice they required from students. With that acknowledgment aside, I asked whether or not *every* student required the same level of practice in order

---

PERSONAL STORY

I had a student in my senior history class a number of years back who never did homework—and I mean *never*. Let's call him Steve. One day, after conducting my usual homework check around the classroom, Steve questioned my behavior.

"Why do you keep asking for my homework?" he asked. "I never have it done, and I don't think I ever will."

In addition to ignoring all his homework assignments, Steve seldom opened his books and was prone to falling asleep in class. Perhaps this was a reflection of my teaching, because he aced every quiz and test—his final exam was exemplary. When measured according to the prescribed learning outcomes of the course, Steve displayed near-universal excellence. During classroom lessons, if my forgetting a key date or struggling to relate a concept happened to coincide with his being awake, he'd bail me out by providing the answer from memory.

Though I did not appreciate Steve's tendency to nod off, and at times I sincerely wished he would just comply with homework regulations, he exemplified a valuable lesson for me: learning outcomes, not behaviors, should be graded. For the first time in my career, I reported a student as needing improvement on class behaviors and work ethic, but as exceptional in terms of meeting learning objectives.

I continued to encourage Steve to display more appropriate classroom behaviors, but stopped using grades as a threatening stick. After a while, I figured I would have to leave it to his summer employer, his parents, or his future college professors to deal with his lack of homework compliance and antisocial behavior. I warned Steve that he might one day need to change his approach to homework.

He left my class with an academic standing of 98 percent. He went on to a full-ride scholarship at college and continued on to a job in international negotiations. We keep in touch to this day.

to grasp a math concept. The answer, of course, was no. Out of this conversation came the interesting question: *could we use homework data, regardless of their origins, to enhance the learning process?*

After pondering the question for a moment, I proposed a framework for comparing homework-completion data to in-class test results in order to determine how much each student's homework-completion rate affects his or her testing success. Upon returning to my own high school I presented this idea to Lisa West, one of our senior math teachers. A few weeks later, she had devised a system for comparing rates of homework completion with corresponding test results that resulted in the nine possible categories shown in Figure 2.3.

This strategy is effective for the following reasons:

1. Learning measures are separated from behavioral ones. Homework completion is a behavioral rather than an academic issue. Students can conceivably ignore their homework entirely and still score very well on tests that measure learning. I have had the pleasure of working with hundreds of educators in North America and Europe, and I have never seen a government policy that required educators to measure rates of homework completion. I have found separating academic measures from behavioral ones to be a breath of fresh air in my classroom. No longer must I sabotage the valuable data that I've accumulated over countless hours of grading legitimate assessments by adding measures of mere compliance to the mix.

2. A personalized learning atmosphere is created. Some students need to do a lot of homework practice to do well; others require much less, or none at all. Many students can personally gauge how much homework they need to do in order to succeed. For students whose poor test scores indicate that they're incapable of managing this, teachers, parents, or administrators can step in to encourage and even mandate better rates of homework completion. If student assessment results are poor in spite of extensive homework efforts, additional interventions may be required. If results are at or above the required level of proficiency with little or no attendant homework

Figure 2.3
Homework-Completion Rates Versus Test Results: The 9 Categories

Category 1: Homework Good/Tests Good
Students who fall into this category generally have learned to do their homework well. They practice their skills at home and are therefore prepared for tests. These students need to continue doing what they're doing.

Category 2: Homework Good/Tests Satisfactory
Students who fall into this category generally try to do most of their homework but either don't ask for help on difficult questions or don't make connections to similar types of questions on tests. They often miss details, gloss over instructions, finish their tests hastily, and make simple mistakes, resulting in test scores that are lower than desired.

Category 3: Homework Good/Tests Poor
Students who fall into this category generally try to complete their homework because they know it needs to be done, but often must rely on notes, classmates, or the teacher to complete it. They tend not go over the homework questions on their own to check for understanding. Some students do not check the answers against the textbook or answer key to make sure they are doing the work correctly. Students in this category are often very anxious about tests and find it hard to communicate what they know on paper. These students need to find a more efficient way to complete their homework while checking for understanding.

Category 4: Homework Satisfactory/Tests Good
Students who fall into this category generally do as much homework as they have time for in class, or do the work necessary to do well on a test. These students often do not have to practice a lot to learn the material well—they tend to learn easily and make connections without extra practice. Students in this category need to be aware that they are responsible for deciding how much homework practice they need to maintain high grades. Such a choice requires sophisticated reasoning.

Category 5: Homework Satisfactory/ Tests Satisfactory
Students who fall into this category generally do as much homework as they have time for in class. Often, they do not answer the last few questions on a given assignment. When students cannot answer questions themselves, they often do not ask for help. These are usually the higher-level thinking questions, and students in this category tend not to answer those correctly on tests. For most students in this category, if they were to complete their homework and ask for help, their test scores would probably improve.

Category 6: Homework Satisfactory/Tests Poor
As with Category 5, students who fall into this category generally do as much homework as they have time for in class, do not answer the last few questions on a given assignment, and tend not to ask for help. Some students answer all the questions but do not check for accuracy. Most students in this category need to apply more effort to answering more questions correctly. It is important for them to focus on what they do and do not know and to ask for help whenever they need it.

Category 7: Homework Poor/Tests Good
Students who fall into this category generally only work on their assignments in class. Their work is often scattered, lost, or completed at random. These students often learn easily and need very little practice; they draw connections during classroom lessons. They often make wise choices about whether or not homework practice will benefit their understanding. Some students do not use class time wisely and are lucky to catch on easily. Students in this category who wish to improve their homework grades need to focus on the details of the concepts being taught.

Category 8: Homework Poor/Tests Satisfactory
Students who fall into this category generally do not use class time wisely to complete their work. They often do not like to take work home, and stop when they get frustrated. Many of them are fine with a satisfactory result, as they are not willing to put forth extra effort. If these students were to complete more of their homework, their test scores would improve. Effort is the key.

Category 9: Homework Poor/Tests Poor
Students who fall into this category generally do not use class time wisely, do not have a habit of completing work, and do not make connections quickly. These are normally the students who need to focus more in class and ask questions about every assignment. More effort and more daily quality work would start to improve their grades and give them added confidence. These students need extra help to make connections every day; they are often students who have struggled throughout their time in school and who have gaps in their background knowledge. Sometimes outside factors contribute to their poor grades. These factors need to be addressed so that students can better concentrate on their work.

effort, students might be encouraged to devote their time and energy to homework for other classes or to hobbies.

3. The teacher becomes an advocate rather than an adversary. For most teachers, homework-completion issues are the root of many negative confrontations with students. The homework-profiling strategy shifts the conversation. Each of the nine profile categories centers on how to help students improve academically given a specific set of variables. As with so many of the other changes I have adopted, homework profiling has not only proven to be more effective at helping students meet learning goals, but also greatly improved my own job satisfaction. Homework completion is now a topic that strengthens my relationships with students rather than eroding them.

Strategy #3: Provide In-School Support

Schools across the world, including my own, are finding money or reinventing supervision schedules in order to set up designated homework rooms. In nearly every case, these supports are in place for students who clearly need to complete homework in order to be successful. During the past four years at Penticton Secondary School, we have developed the following four homework support systems that are independent of the regular class schedule:

1. Lunchtime Homework Room: The teacher delivers a referral sheet to the office, if necessary with a copy of the homework assignment attached to it. An educational assistant is provided with a funded block of time to organize all the referrals and track down each student to verify that he or she plans to attend the support session. In many instances, the educational assistant discovers that the assignment has been completed and helps the student to hand it in. If a student fails to show up to the homework room, a referral is sent to that student's grade-level administrator so that appropriate behavioral consequences and support mechanisms can be introduced.

2. After-School Administrative Support: In this system, an administrator manages the referrals and selected leadership students may provide some of the homework support. Designed for more intensive cases or for students who clearly need to get a little fresh air at lunch, this support is offered in the library after school. It is especially helpful near the end of a reporting period, when some students accumulate incomplete assignments that may directly affect their chances of success on final assessments.

3. Cross-Age Mentoring: As we near exam time, we offer collaborative support sessions in the library, where numerous mentors circle the room and help students complete homework, study for tests, or organize their binders. The largest untapped resource in schools today—older students—are often the mentors. Recent research indicates that cross-age mentoring increases school connectedness, academic achievement, and positive behaviors (Goodwin & Miller, 2012).

4. In-School Suspension: When a student is assigned to in-school suspension (ISS) for a behavioral infraction, the administrator who issued the ISS sends out an electronic form to all teachers, support workers, and counselors who are connected to that student (see Figure 2.4). The teachers respond electronically or in person with homework, tests, or project assignments that the student needs to complete. Providing homework support while a student is serving an in-school suspension seems like a much better solution than traditional suspensions that banish students from the school community. A student who serves a three-day ISS is often able to complete a tremendous amount of homework and can exit the suspension with a better academic standing than before. Our ISS system came about when we had the epiphany that our most at-risk students needed *more* academic and social support from us, not less. As one 9th grader noted after serving his ISS, "Wow, I'm caught up on all my homework! This hasn't happened since, like, 6th grade!"

Strategy #4: Flip Your Classroom

A lot of attention has been paid in recent years to the concept of the flipped classroom. The concept involves having students use online

Figure 2.4
In-School Suspension (ISS) Form

Please fill in all of the applicable fields following the enactment of an In-School Suspension (ISS). Be sure to indicate who has received this e-mail using the last table on this form.

Student name:	
Dates of suspension:	
Grade:	
Administrator in charge of suspension:	

Location of ISS	
	Room 118 Learning Center (Ms. Smith)
	Room 127 Learning Center (Mr. Lennon)
	Room 133 Junior Alternative (Ms. Sanchez)
	Room 210 Senior Alternative (Mr. Anders)
	Room 300 Counseling
	Main Office Area
	Other:

E-Mail Checklist	
	ISS Distribution List: Administrators, counselors, lunch monitor, ISS teacher(s), clerical staff
	Ms. Tracey (youth worker)
	Mr. Sloan (drug and alcohol intervention)
	All classroom teachers of the ISS student

Thank you for your support,

The ISS Team

Source: Courtesy Doug Scotchburn. Used with permission.

resources to experience lessons at home, then practice what they've learned in the classroom—an inversion of the conventional lessons-at-school/practice-at-home format. Increasingly, teachers are producing their own 6- to 8-minute videos for this purpose and uploading them to the web. Educators champion this rather new idea as a way to increase the contact between students and teachers. The classroom transforms from a place of static lecture to a buzzing hive of energizing activity. When the content is delivered at home, the classroom can be used to explore extension activities, conduct small-group learning exercises, and provide homework support for students who most need it.

A note about the use of technology to further student learning: I recently attended a presentation by Scott McLeod, a University of Kentucky professor, author, blogger, and the force behind the *Shift Happens* DVD series. His message at the 2011 NESA Conference in Athens, Greece, was simultaneously troubling and exciting: namely, that schools must adopt online cloud technology to facilitate the flow of information or risk withering away into extinction. McLeod contends that a shift comparable to that brought on by the printing press is upon us now that information is free, readily available, and impossible to contain. He questions the practice of buying regular textbooks and of traditional lecture-based delivery models. Though he did not discuss homework in particular, I suspect that homework will not be isolated from this trend toward information decentralization. Students can access a virtually limitless universe of fact-based information at any time from any place equipped with a Wi-Fi or data network. Such information could prove incredibly valuable as long as we recognize it as a *support* for learning rather than *evidence* of learning.

Conclusion

Homework can be the key to academic success for one student, and seemingly a waste of time for another. To understand the role of homework, it is critical first to determine the extent to which it is needed for each student, and then to ensure that students are completing the work themselves. Homework assignments should provide students with an opportunity to practice what they're learning in the classroom. It is a tool in the learning process, not an instrument to measure understanding.

After presenting some of my homework changes at a conference in Idaho a few summers ago, a teacher interrupted me to ask a simple question: "It seems like you must not have a lot of homework to grade. Is that true?" After assuring her that I had greatly reduced my grading load at home, she began to cry. The room went quiet as we listened to her explain that she had so much work to grade that she was losing touch with her family and on the verge of switching careers. She had always believed that everything her students completed needed to find its way into the grade book. Finally, she had found an alternative.

Frequently Asked Questions

Q: I want to offer homework supports, but my school administration is not interested in designing a system for the whole school. I don't want to give up every one of my lunch sessions to do it on my own. What do you suggest?

A: Offering homework support each day can be very draining. If administrative support is lacking, one alternative is to gather smaller groups to form homework-support systems. Here are some examples:

- A team of 7th grade teachers establishes a schedule whereby each teacher manages a homework-completion center one day per week. Because the center is in a different room each day, the team develops a schedule that is easy for students to remember (e.g., Mondays with Ms. Mitchell, Tuesdays in 211).
- At the high school I worked at, I was one of two social studies teachers who offered systematic homework support to students: I would open my classroom up on Mondays and Wednesdays, and

my colleague, Mr. Reid, took Tuesdays and Thursdays. We felt that we were often picking up the pieces from students who were unable to get subject-specific support elsewhere in the school.

Q: How will parents react if I start assigning less homework?

A: Because parents may initially be alarmed at the reduction in homework, it is important to communicate clearly with them that homework will be assigned on the basis of each student's individual needs. Communication is critical not only to explain the system, but also to let parents know how in-class results are shaping up for their kids. Parents will be alarmed if quiz and test scores are lower than anticipated, so reacting quickly and effectively is critical if your changes are to be perceived as effective. Low test scores are quite possibly an indicator that more homework practice is necessary.

Q: Do some students ask for more homework?

A: Yes! Some students are used to getting regular homework assignments and may feel uneasy about losing a system that they perceived to be working for them. I try to frame conversations with students around the value of purposeful and engaging work. Just because something has been effective doesn't mean that it's the right thing to do or even the best alternative. History is full of examples of systems that garnered the sought-after results, but their methods turned out to be less than optimal for the people involved. I suggest that students engage in extension activities, long-term projects, or pointed investigations. Having resources on hand that push students to learn more is a better approach than assigning work that they have already mastered just to keep them busy.

Q: Does assigning less homework leave students underprepared for postsecondary education?

A: I have heard from former students who have gone on to postsecondary school and who have told me that they were perfectly ready. Still, there is no question that college is very different from high school. Some students find that their success with homework completion in high school doesn't translate to success in college, where writing papers and engaging in critical research are paramount. I have seen little in the way of uniform homework assignments that would help in these areas. Instructors at the postsecondary level need students who can engage in critical thinking, who can apply skills and knowledge to novel scenarios, and who are open to new ideas and concepts.

3

UNIT PLANS

If you don't know where you are going,
you will probably end up somewhere else.

—Lawrence J. Peter

Most people want to know where they are going and what plans are in store for them when they get there. Two separate studies have shown that people in fact gain more joy from planning a trip than from taking the trip itself (Mitchell, Thompson, Peterson, & Cronk, 1997; Nawijn, Marchand, Veenhoven, & Vingerhoets, 2010). Teachers also like to plan in advance: I certainly wanted to know my teaching assignment months ahead of time so that I could start wrapping my head around the courses I'd be delivering. If I happened to remember

PERSONAL STORY

When I first began handing out unit plans in class, I was unsure whether they were of much value to my students. Was I needlessly draining my photocopy budget by supplying every student with a hard copy of the plan? To settle the matter, one morning I asked my students if they thought I should continue supplying them with unit plans. Morgan, a quiet student who seldom spoke, felt prompted to share her views.

"These unit plans are awesome!" she said. "I mean, I get to figure out what I know and don't know before I even write the test."

Tiana was quick to agree. "I am able to focus my studying and save time. Between my job, a heavy course load, my boyfriend, and the girls' volleyball team, I need all the help I can get making my study time more efficient."

Andre's opinion was the most direct: "If you stop giving out these unit plans, I'm screwed."

that we were having a staff meeting, I felt more comfortable seeing the agenda beforehand. As a volleyball coach, I wanted my tournament schedule set before the season started so that I could chart a proper training pace for my players. Maybe it's just human nature—we crave some element of predictability and find comfort in knowing a little about the future. If this is true of trips, tournaments, and meetings, it's even more so of teaching.

It should come as no surprise that students also appreciate knowing what is in store for them in a unit of study. In my first semester at university, I was shocked when a professor handed out potential exam questions a week in advance of the testing date. At the start of the second semester, I nearly fell off my chair when another professor gave us a detailed course agenda *and* our final exam questions on the first day of class. One thing became immediately clear: there was no way that I would ever be able to claim that I did not know what was expected of me. I have since found that everyone benefits when the mystery is removed and learning objectives are clearly stated.

The Trouble with Surprises

I used to think that it was critical for the sake of academic rigor to subject my students to surprises, especially in testing situations. I would swell with pride if some element of my test were cloaked in enough secrecy to elicit beads of sweat from even my strongest students. I recall being smugly vague and intentionally ambiguous as my students asked questions about upcoming test details.

Though I have since come to see surprise as an element best kept away from test situations, I know I am not the only educator who has at some point felt otherwise. I have heard teachers boast that they introduced their students to a new topic *on the test itself.* I have even seen a teacher rub his hands with glee because he knew that his students would soon realize, while taking a test, that they'd overlooked a certain concept in their studies. Astonishingly, this teacher seemed to accept little responsibility for his students' oversight.

Teachers should want to encourage *positive transfer*—that is, the enhancement of learning in one context because of learning acquired in another context—but perhaps not on tests and exams. Unit tests should measure student learning of material explicitly covered in class and should not be used as tools of surprise. I believe that my former strategy of surprising my students on test day frustrated the most capable learners and discouraged the most vulnerable.

For most of my teaching career, I would start lessons by simply talking about the material to my class with as much enthusiasm as I could muster. Sometimes I'd employ a hook such as an engaging movie scene or shocking image to get the conversation started. But as much as I tried to fill the learning environment with a sense of anticipation, I now realize that the road ahead remained foggy to my students, despite my best intentions. They didn't know where the lesson was taking them, and I found it hard to convey to them the clear sense of direction that I had in my head.

A recent study at the Free University of Amsterdam showed how obstructing an observable target can affect our perception of its size (Anderson, 2011). Subjects in the study were asked to putt a golf ball into a cup from about five feet away. Each golfer was allowed to freely examine the cup before attempting to hit the target. When it came time to putt, the golfers were divided into three groups: one with no obstructions between the subjects and the target, one that had to thread the ball between two obstacles en route to the hole, and one that had to putt the ball under a curtain that obstructed the target completely. After each putt, the subject was asked to estimate the size of the target on a computer screen. The results showed an inverse relationship between the perceived size of the target and the degree of obstruction: in general, the more obstructed the view, the smaller the target was perceived to be. Perhaps this study has implications for learning targets. Students might perceive them to be more attainable if they have a clear idea of what they are and can access them whenever they need to.

Strategies for Ensuring That Students Know the Road Ahead

The following strategies can help ensure that students understand how to use the unit plans to effectively tackle a variety of learning activities.

Strategy #1: Deliver Student-Friendly Unit Plans

Every unit of study includes different types of learning targets and different methods for demonstrating capacity. In my experience, there are three critical steps to building an effective unit plan. First, it is essential to determine which types of targets students will be asked to meet. Chappuis, Stiggins, Chappuis, and Arter (2012) have devised the following four categories of learning targets:

- Knowledge targets (What do I need to know?)
- Reasoning targets (What can I do with what I know?)
- Skill targets (What can I demonstrate?)
- Product targets (What can I make to show my learning?)

The second step to building an effective unit plan is to populate each category. For example, during the unit, you may have students first recount what they know, then demonstrate the skills they've acquired based on that knowledge, or you may ask them to reason through a dilemma using the knowledge they've learned. The third step is to present each target as an "I can" statement, as this makes it easier for students to take ownership of the targets. I have come to believe that "I can" statements help students to realize the importance of personal growth. They also set the expectation that students will be graded according to their own learning continua rather than against their classmates (O'Connor, 2010).

Knowledge Targets: All fact-based objectives belong in this category: definitions, dates, names, and other specific information that students need to *know*. It is important to explain to students that knowledge targets are the essential building blocks of the unit. Just as having all ingredients is critical to completing a recipe, it is necessary to have core knowledge in place in order to succeed with higher-order tasks. A good unit plan reflects Bloom's taxonomy, with knowledge at the lower end of the spectrum and reasoning at the higher end. For example, a knowledge target for a unit on the run-up to World War II might read as follows: *I can list four conditions in 1930s Germany that resulted in Hitler gaining power.*

Reasoning Targets: Any targets that relate to what students can *do* with what they know belong in this category. These targets are often more engaging than knowledge targets, as students are required to bring disparate pieces of knowledge together to form an argument or make a judgment. Command terms such as *to what extent, justify, determine, compare,* and *evaluate* are commonly found in this category. The best reasoning targets encourage students to take ownership of their responses. Be sure to draw the connection between knowledge and reasoning targets for students; they need to realize that solid reasoning consists of knowledge used strategically and in context. A reasoning target from the unit on the run-up to World War II might read as follows: *I can explain how the United States followed a policy of isolationism in the 1930s.*

Skill Targets: Here the focus is on what students can do to *demonstrate* understanding—delivering a speech to the class, for example, or designing a map. A skills target from the unit on the run-up to World War II might read as follows: *I can research a member of the Jewish community from 1930s Germany and give a two-minute speech on his/her specific concerns or challenges.* Many homework assignments fit into this category as well. Here's an example of a geography skill target from a unit on the American Revolution that I taught: *I can arrange the 13 colonies in the correct geographical order.* To engage in a formative assessment in class, I gave students 13 pieces of paper, each of which represented a colony, and had them arrange them in the proper order. The same activity could be used for placing events in chronological order. In mathematics, this activity could easily be modified to create a number line indicating the relative values of fractions. Regardless of the subject area, it is beneficial for students to practice formative, skill-based activities at home in preparation for tests. Practicing skill-based activities can help students to entrench knowledge.

The relationship between practice and knowledge is inescapable. How can a student deliver a persuasive speech on the challenges faced by German Jews in the 1930s without the necessary background knowledge? It is impossible for students to meet reasoning and skill targets without first having the knowledge in place. By performing a speech to the class, a student further processes and embeds the knowledge required for the speech.

Product Targets: Virtually anything that a student might *make* to show his or her learning belongs in this category, including final projects. Here's an example: *I can produce a collage of images that represent the social conditions of German Jews in the 1930s.* Product targets can include posters, paragraphs, slide show presentations, and most anything else that students might create. Knowing that my students typically referred to their unit plan throughout a unit, I began handing out more detailed guidelines for product targets. Here are two examples:

Example 1: *I can write a one- to two-page reflection on my experience at our own Paris Peace Conference. My written assignment will incorporate the following topics:*

A. My overall impression of the experience.

B. What I found frustrating or successful about the experience.

C. How the process affected my understanding of the difficulties associated with war guilt, colonialism, self-determination, and the prevention of future wars.

Example 2: *I can construct a clay 3-D model depicting our solar system. My model will include the following components:*

A. The sun and all of the planets in our solar system.

B. A scale reflecting the relative sizes of the planets.

C. Details for each planet, including approximate color and distance from other planets.

D. The location and relative size of the asteroid belt.

As these examples suggest, there is value in letting students know the basic requirements for meeting each target in advance. Listing the requirements in the plan makes it easy for students to access the information when they need to. You might even consider printing the unit plan on a certain color of paper so that it stands out in students' binders.

The research supporting the use of clear learning targets is overwhelming. O'Connor (2010), Reeves (2010), and Wiliam (2011), among others, have established that students learn better when they clearly understand their learning targets. Both teachers and students benefit immensely when clear targets are matched to student performance. As Moss and Brookhart (2012) note,

> A strong target-performance match translates the learning target into action. Engaged in a strong performance of understanding, students should be able to conclude, "If I can do this, then I will know I have reached the learning target." Just as important, teachers should be able to conclude, "If my students can do this, then I will have strong evidence that they have reached the learning target." (p. 44)

My students have reacted very positively to unit plans featuring learning targets, even using them as study guides at the end of each unit. Students welcomed the plans because they could see what was required of them in order to succeed on unit tests. Though I had initially intended to start with a unit plan for a single course and assess its efficacy before designing others, it didn't take long for me to realize that I wouldn't be stopping at one. My students soon became accustomed to getting a unit plan at the start of each unit and immediately seeing both the micro and macro learning objectives in store. They came to rely on unit plans to gauge their progress, both individually and as a class, as we covered each topic.

Here are some reasons why student-friendly unit plans with learning targets encourage student success:

1. The unit plans align with the test. It is valuable to design unit plans with the end of the unit in mind. Many teachers already possess good unit tests, and a matching unit plan can prepare students for them; a good unit plan makes a great study guide. The challenge is to design a plan that contains both the critical knowledge pieces and any reasoning targets that could potentially be asked on the test so that students can prepare for every possible test question. Teachers who are new to the profession or who are preparing to deliver a new course are advised to design their plans prior to designing unit tests and basing them on the learning objectives established by the school system. Such unit plans will form the basis of sound assessments.

2. The unit plans offer students ownership through student-friendly language. A student who approaches an "I can" prompt with the goal of determining whether or not he or she really can meet the stated target is taking part in a formative assessment exercise. This proactive approach to test preparation is exactly what I had long encouraged my students to do, and the unit plans supplied them with the essential tools to do it. To make unit plans more effective and welcoming, reword the learning objectives set out by the school system. As a rule, the younger the student, the more the learning objectives should be broken down into manageable pieces. As an example, consider the following reasoning objective taken from the Texas state standards for science: *"Describe producer/consumer, predator/prey, and parasite/host relationships as they occur in food webs within marine, freshwater, and terrestrial ecosystems"* (Texas Education Agency, 2011). You might break down this objective into knowledge and reasoning targets as follows:

Knowledge Targets

- I can <u>define</u> the following terms as they relate to our unit:

consumer	**host**	**prey**
ecosystem	**marine**	**producer**
food webs	**parasite**	**relationships**
freshwater	**predator**	**terrestrial**

- I know what is meant by the term <u>describe</u> and I can apply it to scientific topics.

Reasoning Targets

- I can <u>describe</u> the relationships as they occur in food webs between a **producer** and **consumer** in each of the following ecosystems: **freshwater, marine,** and **terrestrial.**
- I can <u>describe</u> the relationships as they occur in food webs between a **predator** and its **prey** in each of the following ecosystems: **freshwater, marine,** and **terrestrial.**
- I can <u>describe</u> the relationships as they occur in food webs between a **parasite** and **host** in each of the following ecosystems: **freshwater, marine,** and **terrestrial.**

Formatting the unit plan carefully can really help students. Use bold for key terms and consider isolating them at the beginning of the knowledge section. Students may find it helpful if command terms such as *compare, contrast, describe, discuss,* and *evaluate* are underlined or highlighted. Whatever formatting method you choose, remember that your goal is to help students better understand what is expected of them.

3. Unit plans are tailored for different subject areas. The extent to which each category of learning target is used will depend upon the subject area, though knowledge targets should be used extensively in most. For example, a plan for a unit on tennis in P.E. class might include knowledge targets asking students to describe the rules of the game and the use of equipment, and skill targets asking them to demonstrate serves and strokes, but no reasoning or product targets at all. Though reasoning and product targets are often left out of P.E. plans, with a little imagination and creativity, they could be added—by asking students to construct "how-to" brochures on the basic swings in tennis, for example, or to film a video on the benefits of tennis. (Throw in a few cheesy tennis outfits and you've suddenly got a great intro video for next year's class!)

Strategy #2: Use Unit Plans Throughout the Learning Process

I have found that unit plans are best applied starting on day one of the unit and continuing through to the final test date (and sometimes even beyond). I encourage students to place their plans at the front of the section for the unit in their binders or as the front page of a digital portfolio. I typically go over the unit plan with my students on day one and refer to it over the course of the unit. Before the final unit test, I encourage students to use the plan as a study guide. Karl Koehler, a math teacher and the principal of Atascocita Middle School in Humble, Texas, has created one of the best examples of a unit plan I have ever seen (see Figure 3.1). His incorporation of various formative assessment features is exemplary.

Here are some reasons for employing a unit plan from the very beginning and through the very end of a unit:

1. Unveiling unit plans early on can uncover levels of background knowledge and possible resources for use in the class. If teachers were ever the keepers of all knowledge, this certainly is no

Figure 3.1
Factors and Multiples Unit Plan

Name: _____   Teacher: _____

Will breaking a number into factors help me solve a problem? What do factors and multiples of numbers tell me about a situation?

Knowledge Targets *"What do I need to know?"*	1. I can explain the difference between a factor and a multiple.
	2. I can identify factors of a positive integer. **6.1E**
	3. I can identify common factors and the greatest common factor (GCF) of two or more positive integers. **6.1E**
	4. I can identify multiples of a positive integer. **6.1F**
	5. I can identify common multiples and the least common multiple (LCM) of two or more positive integers. **6.1F**
	6. I can identify a set of positive integers. **6.1F**
Skill Targets *"What can I demonstrate?"*	7. I can solve real-life problems that require using LCM or GCF.
	8. I can use multiplication of whole numbers to solve problems including situations involving equivalent ratios and rates. **6.2C**
	9. I can use division of whole numbers to solve problems including situations involving equivalent ratios and rates. **6.2C**

Every composite number has a unique "fingerprint"— an expression as a product of prime numbers unique only to that number, regardless of order of the factors.

What is my academic goal for this unit?

Summative Assessments:

1 **Just starting,** Insufficient	2 **Yes, but . . . ,** Minimal	3 **Yes,** Proficient	4 **WOW!** Excellent
Less than 60% accurate	Between 60 and 74% accurate	Between 75 and 89% accurate	90% or greater
Not able to explain math process or explain key math points	Able to show process, but not able to identify/explain key math points	Able to both explain process and identify/explain key math points	Able to explain key math points accurately in a variety of problems

(cont.)

Figure 3.1 CONTINUED
Factors and Multiples Unit Plan

Learning Target	Assignment	Target/Goal	Your Rubric Score	Met Standard/ Target?

| factor | common factor | greatest common factor (GCF) | prime number | composite number |
| multiple | common multiple | least common multiple (LCM) | prime factorization | factor pair |

Source: Karl Koehler, Atascocita Middle School, Humble, Texas. Used with permission.

longer the case. Information today is free and readily available. There is a pretty good chance that my students have heard of World War II prior to arriving in my classroom. My son began collecting and classifying insects before he got to kindergarten. The fact that students bring past knowledge and experiences to the classroom is just one of the reasons why it's beneficial to cover the scope of a unit early in the process. Unveiling the unit plan helps you to adjust the way you cover a unit based on the extent to which students are already familiar with the topic.

One simple way to encourage early conversations about the material is to ask each student to underline five terms or concepts from the unit plan with which he or she is already familiar. If the student is unfamiliar with all of the terms or concepts, ask him or her to predict what they might mean. Then, ask each student to select a partner with whom to compare past experiences and knowledge. Circulate around the class and listen in on these dialogues. I have found it helpful to engage in some of the conversations myself as a way of gaining some insight into the competencies that each student is bringing to the table.

The extent to which students already know the material can guide future activities. Perhaps a critical topic has already been covered in the previous grade and needn't be covered in great detail. Or maybe students from a particular feeder school or who attended a particular class are already familiar with some of the material, in which case you might provide them with an extension activity to reduce boredom and classroom disruption while you teach the material to the rest of the class.

Sometimes these initial conversations may serve as a barometer of individual students' cultural sensitivities and help to uncover relevant resources that students may have at their disposal. Here's an example. One year, on the day that I introduced a unit on the Cold War, one of my students approached me after class and suggested that I might want to call her grandfather, who had immigrated to Canada after fighting the communists in the Hungarian Revolution. I did as she suggested and set up an in-class interview with the man. His insights and personal experiences gave my students a far deeper understanding of the topic than they otherwise would have had.

2. Unit plans grant students ongoing access to, and a sense of ownership of, the learning process. Road maps are used not only to plot the initial stages of a journey, but also to help us during the trip. The same is true for unit plans. During each lesson, it is a good idea for students to have access to the learning targets so that they can stay on track and achieve the critical understanding that is the purpose of the unit. Teachers, too, should refer back to the unit plan as they plot students' progress through the unit. Unit plans help students to know when their unit tests are approaching and can serve as detailed itineraries of expected learning outcomes. One lasting benefit of unit plans is that they allow students to feel as though they are a part of the effective management of the learning process.

3. Unit plans help students to assess their own competency. For many years, I encouraged my students to study at home before they took in-class tests. I'd suggest that they make up questions and see if they could answer them to determine their readiness. Though my intentions were good, I realize now that most students did not know how to construct an easy-to-use, at-home study guide. My suggestion did more to absolve me of responsibility than to help students in their educational journey. As I developed my first few unit plans, it dawned on me that the test-making professional in the room was finally doing his job properly. With a well-designed unit plan, students preparing for a test can check off the boxes beside each learning target as they determine their own aptitude. If students are unsure whether their responses to learning targets are adequate, you can encourage them to hand in sample responses in the days leading up to the test, either individually or as a whole class.

The feedback I got from students after designing my very first unit plan was encouraging. One student said it helped her to focus on her studying and figure out what she did and didn't know before the test; another concurred and added that it helped her to save time studying. Since then, on a few occasions, students have informed me that we overlooked an element listed on the plan in our lesson. In one instance, a fire drill interrupted us during class, and I neglected to return to the unfinished lesson when it was over. Near the end of that unit, a student identified the knowledge target that I hadn't gotten to on the day of the drill, and we were able to address it before the test. Clearly, a comprehensive unit plan can serve as a safety net for such situations.

Strategy #3: Incorporate Student Examples in Unit Plans and Have Students Assess One Another's Work

At a recent conference, I heard a teacher take the position that students should not be allowed to see examples from previous years of projects that they'll be asked to complete. When I asked her why, she explained that such examples compromised students' "original thought." I disagree. This seems to me like one of those arbitrary rules found only in schools. When my wife and I recently decided to renovate the exterior of our home, we spent many hours touring housing developments for ideas. Examples usually result in improvements on, rather than mere replications of, what currently exists.

Allowing students to discuss the qualities and characteristics of preexisting projects leads to valuable conversations and skill development. Furthermore, by inviting students to comment on examples from previous years, we are giving them a taste of what it means to assess student work. Students will best process the criteria that they themselves need to meet if they are first asked to assess someone else's work. One very effective technique is to display an example of a completed project and challenge students to reverse-engineer it. According to Jarrod Diamond (1997), the mere act of observing a U.S. nuclear explosion in 1947 likely allowed the Soviet Union to develop a nuclear weapon faster than it would have otherwise, probably by taking a series of different steps than the United States did.

As Wiliam (2011) notes, "Ensuring that all students know what quality work looks like has a profound impact on achievement gaps" (p. 55). If you don't have previous examples of student work on a project, find some online or construct one yourself to give students a good idea of what is required. Some of your students' projects may end up being similar to the examples, but if the examples are of high quality, this is a *good* thing.

All members of the learning community are capable of assessing learning outcomes, including students. In fact, students form one of the largest untapped resources in schools today. In addition to reviewing examples of previous student work, you may want to have your students assess one another's projects as well. As most parents can attest, a single word from a child's classmate can have more of an impact than a million words from a grown-up's mouth. If there is truth to the aphorism, "It takes a village to raise a child," why don't we let the youngest community members in on assessment?

Following are a few examples of ways to include students in the assessment process. (It bears mentioning that all of these assessments are purely formative—the results will not make up any part of the student's official academic standing.)

Rubrics: Rubrics are an incredibly effective tool for assessment when used properly. In her book *How to Create and Use Rubrics for Formative Assessment and Grading* (2013), Susan Brookhart offers the following guidelines about rubrics:

- The main purpose of a rubric is to assess performances. Shooting a basketball, delivering a speech, and producing a poster or essay all constitute different types of performance. Rubrics are *not* normally focused on tasks, quotas, or behaviors.
- Rubrics have two distinct elements: (1) a clear and understandable set of criteria, and (2) descriptions of different levels of performance.
- The performance-level descriptions on rubrics should be based on the unit's established learning outcomes.
- Rubrics are not designed to judge; they are designed to assess.

I regularly ask students to use rubrics to peer- and self-assess projects or major components of projects. When students use rubrics to self-assess their own performances, the chances that they will truly process and understand the criteria listed on the rubric increase. I believe it is important for students to view their own work through the lens of the performance-level descriptions on rubrics. Rubrics are fantastic formative assessment tools, as they provide students with the opportunity to identify areas needing improvement before the final grading stage. It can be very valuable for students to pair up and assess each other's projects using rubrics.

Interactive Unit Plans: Unit plans can be formatted to include room for students to actually demonstrate their understanding of the material as well as for peer assessment. In these cases, consider using different-colored ink to differentiate among student, peer, and teacher remarks. I learned from my friend and colleague Chris Bradley that including a place for students to add their initials on these types of unit plans subtly increases student responsibility, accountability, and owner-ship. An example of one of Chris's plans can be seen in Figure 3.2.

The Sticky Walk: Place student projects around the classroom for all to clearly see, then ask students to walk around the room and place sticky notes on or near each project. The sticky notes may con-tain comments, suggestions, or questions relating to each project. This activity can be used with virtually any type of project but is especially powerful with those that have strong visual components (e.g., photo-graphs, pottery, paintings).

Student Planning Stations: Before starting a project, have stu-dents complete a plan outlining how they intend to meet the project's learning targets. Tell students that they will be pitching their project plans to a producer in hopes of securing a deal for a TV show, book, or other type of product line. Once the students have all completed their plans, ask them to form pairs and share their plans with their partners. One person in each pair is designated an "agent" and the other is designated a "producer." (You may want to choose alternative titles that are age or course appropriate.) Give each agent a set amount of time—say, two to four minutes—to explain his or her project plan, what he or she is most looking forward to, and precisely how he or she intends to address the learning targets. Then, allow the producer the same amount of time to ask clarification questions focused on how the learning outcomes will be presented. Once the producer is done, have students switch roles to address the second project plan.

Conclusion

We all want to know where we are going and how we might best get there. Surprises can be fun and exhilarating, but when the stakes are

Figure 3.2
Sample Interactive Unit Plan

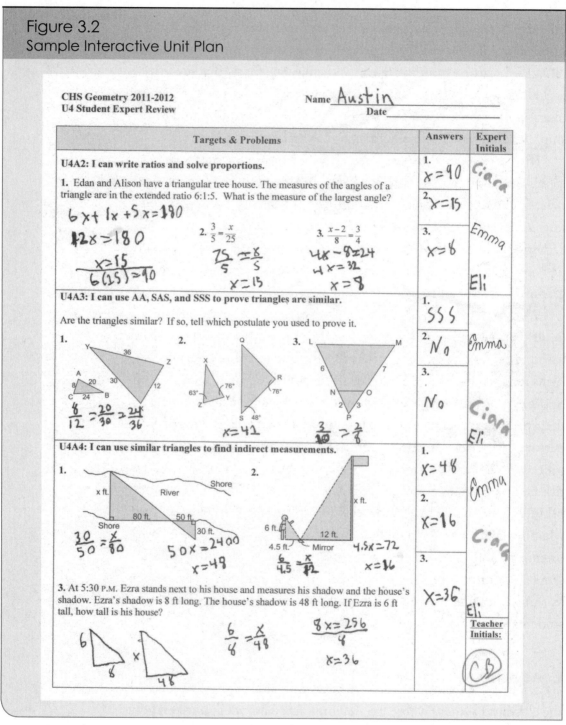

Source: Courtesy Chris Bradley. Used with permission.

high, predictability is helpful. My students have responded so favorably to unit plans that they'll ask for them if I neglect to hand them out. I make my plans available to parents electronically, and have found that they are quick to access them to see what is required of their children in my class.

Presenting students with a clear sense of direction has improved my job satisfaction. I take great joy in seeing struggling learners become more confident and assured, and I myself am more comfortable when I've formalized the learning path into a clear plan. The clearer the path to success—especially if that success is going to be measured—the happier I am, and the same holds true for my students.

Frequently Asked Questions

Q: What if some students don't use the unit plans?

A: I find that a small percentage of students tend not to use the unit plans at all, so I focus on the feedback from those who do. If some students are not using the unit plans successfully, look for ways to encourage them to use them as formative assessment tools. I strongly suggest carefully going over the first unit plan that you give to a class. The time you invest in patiently analyzing and explaining the first plan will not only increase the likelihood that your students will use it, but will also save time when you administer later unit plans. If you find that a significant number of plans are being wasted or if your photocopying resources are limited, consider posting the plans online or distributing them by e-mail.

Q: I struggle to distinguish between knowledge targets and reasoning targets. Do you have any advice?

A: I tend to use the command terms as my guide. Terms that elicit factual evidence, such as *define, list, identify,* and *name,* suggest knowledge targets. By contrast, terms that require students to make a judgment of some sort, such as *justify, evaluate, to what extent,* and *argue,* suggest reasoning targets. Another indicator is that knowledge targets must be met before reasoning targets can be met.

Q: If a student gives a speech or other presentation to the class, does it qualify as a skill or a product?

A: I try to separate the action from the product. Delivering a speech is a skill, whereas the script or notes for the speech are a product. Look closely at the prescribed learning outcomes: if public speaking is not prescribed, I wouldn't grade the skill piece, but rather ask students to use the speech as a tool to reflect and focus on another learning out-come. As I've said previously, *you should only grade what you are asked to by the learning standards.*

Q: How long does it take to create a unit plan?

A: This is a tricky question. My usual answer is, "Not as long as I thought it would." Each unit plan gets easier than the one before. Once you've got a template and you're accustomed to using it, the process becomes a matter of populating sections based on command terms.

Q: I don't have time to make unit plans for each subject I teach. What can I do?

A: Start with one unit in one course. If you ask and receive valuable feedback from students on the plan, continue developing plans for each subsequent unit. By starting small, you will learn from the process and avoid making the same mistakes on all your plans. If you have col-leagues who teach the same course, ask them if they'd be interested in collaborating on unit plans. You can either build each plan together or divide the workload and share the results. I have seen both approaches used effectively.

Q: Compared to other grading and assessment changes, how important are student-friendly unit plans?

A: I believe in starting at the beginning with the end in mind. Designing student-friendly unit plans is a natural first step to developing capacity for assessment. The process benefits all major stakeholders: students, parents, support workers, counselors, and teachers. Once the learning path is clear and the necessary components are identified, you can move on to helping students meet their learning targets.

Q: Can unit plans be used at any age level?

A: Assuming that students benefit from knowing what is expected of them, the answer is yes. For younger students, simplify learning targets and separate them into smaller pieces.

Q: Have struggling learners reacted negatively to your unit plans?

A: Yes. Some struggling learners have been overwhelmed by unit plans with a lot of targets. Such plans can intimidate learners who have low academic self-esteem. One solution to this problem is to split the unit into two smaller units, or to split the plan into two parts. I now have a rule that I will divide a unit plan in two if it can't fit onto two easy-to-read pages.

Q: What exceptional behaviors have you seen that stem from your adoption of unit plans?

A: Rarely, I've found that some very high-functioning students, especially ones who suffer from immense academic pressures to succeed, try to meet the learning targets ahead of the lessons. There is nothing inherently wrong with this, as the students are simply aiming to perform at an exceptional level. At most, it can get a little annoying when students ask for clarification about targets that we've yet to discuss as a class. In these cases, I encourage students to be patient.

4

RETESTING

> I don't offer retests. There is no such thing as a retest.
> Tests cease to be tests if students
> can just do them over again.
>
> *—Myron Dueck, circa 1998*

In the first 10 years of my teaching career, whenever the topic of retesting arose, I was always among the first to shoot it down. I firmly believed that the tests I administered were not just assessing my students' learning, but also measuring and helping to entrench such valuable attributes as a good work ethic, the ability to concentrate, strong study skills, self-motivation, compliance with rules, and effective communication skills. To erode the value of tests by allowing students to retake them seemed to me nothing short of absurd.

It turns out that I was not alone in rejecting the notion of retesting. Gabriel Rshaid (2011), author of *Learning for the Future,* acknowledges the existence of both evidence for, and resistance against, the practice:

> Despite years of educational seminars, hundreds of books dedicated to breaking down the nature and goals of assessment, and a clearly discernible movement towards formative assessment, the vast majority of assessments in school systems all over the world and in every age group are still sit-down, fixed-time, end-of-unit written tests with no second chances. (p. 25)

In December 2006, at a grading conference in Portland, Oregon, I heard Rick Stiggins present the idea that students should be able to answer the following three critical questions during any learning phase:

1. Where am I going?
2. Where am I now?
3. How can I close the gap?

At the time, I believed that well-designed unit plans such as those discussed in Chapter 3 would do a fine job of helping students to answer the first question, and that my students would be able to answer the second question as they always had, by reviewing their graded tests along with my descriptive feedback. However, the third question— How can I close the gap?—caused me discomfort. If a student knew what he or she needed to learn (Where am I going?) and how close he or she had come to learning it (Where am I now?), the next and final hurdle was to determine how to master what hadn't been learned. I realized that I wasn't addressing this last step adequately in my classroom. I did not have a system in place to help students address the learning they had missed (or the teaching I had failed to deliver). If a student scored 78 percent on a unit test, there was no way to address the other 22 percent. Clearly, I would need to restructure my approach to testing. On leaving the conference, I made up my mind to design a way for students to show the learning they had accomplished *during* or *after* the testing process.

When I initially decided to offer my students retests, I did not know that I was about to embark on a journey that would fundamentally change the classroom experience for both me and my students. I also didn't realize that I would end up restructuring my entire assessment system. I thought that I could administer retests using my existing system; I figured it would just be a matter of asking a few more topical questions on retests. I hoped to avoid having to construct entirely new tests. It would not take long for these hopes to be dashed.

I clearly remember the first time I offered retests to a class of seniors. Upon returning a set of tests to my students, I announced with some trepidation that they could have a retest if they were unhappy with their results; they simply had to drop by after class and arrange a retesting date. One of my students, Allie, requested a retest, and we arranged a lunch meeting for the following day. In advance of the meeting, I reviewed Allie's test and tried to determine how best to conduct the retest. The test consisted of a few sections, and Allie requested that the retest focus only on the first section of 40 multiple-choice questions, 12 of which she had gotten wrong. Given the complexity of the questions and the fact that they reflected a variety of different learning objectives and topics, I found it hard to ascertain where, specifically, Allie's weaknesses lay. Compounding the difficulty was the fact that multiple-choice questions make it hard to determine how *close* a student is to the correct answer.

I considered asking Allie to complete a new multiple-choice section filled with a random selection of questions from the unit. However, because the original section addressed a variety of learning targets, this approach did not seem a suitable replacement for the initial assessment. In any event, I did not have a second set of 40 multiple-choice questions ready to serve as a retest. I decided instead to have a conversation with Allie about each of the original questions that she'd gotten wrong to determine if she had gained a better understanding of the underlying concepts. If she had, I was ready to modify her original score. This approach proved ineffective: after discussing the questions for about 30 minutes, neither of us could tell whether she knew the material any better than before. The unavoidable conclusion was that I needed to create an efficient retesting system from scratch.

Problems with Traditional Classroom Testing Systems

Traditional classroom testing systems are built upon the flawed notion that tests cannot be revisited. As best as I can recall, my own schooling experience was totally devoid of retests. I would imagine that this is the case for most teachers, suggesting that we tend to replicate the systems from which we advance. Since adopting retests in my classroom, I have had a lot of people inform me that retests don't prepare students for "the real world." As one friend told me very early in my retesting venture, "You have to understand, Myron: I own a small company, and in the real world you only have one shot at things, so you'd better get them right the first time." Having worked in schools all my life, I was clearly in need of some enlightenment, so I asked my friend to give me an example of a situation in "the real world" where someone might take a formal test and not be allowed a retest. After a long silence, my friend admitted that she couldn't think of one. Certainly, there are testlike moments that can't be done over—sports tournaments, for example. Still, I have yet to hear of an instance in the real world where a formal test cannot be retaken. As Rshaid (2011) puts it,

> Our educational system is supposed to prepare students for real life, and it is easy to see that this artificial assessment model has little resemblance to reality. In real life there are almost no one-chance do-or-die scenarios, and whenever anybody has to demonstrate proficiency in any field, the timing for demonstrating that competency is chosen by the candidate rather than being an arbitrary date set in stone. (p. 26)

Tests Are Snapshots in Time

The standard unit test is an indicator of someone's ability at a single moment in time. As such, outcomes can be affected by variables totally unrelated to the learning targets. Sometimes these factors are self-imposed, and sometimes they lie entirely outside of students' control. Students have little control over test times and dates, for example, so if they happen to have a fight or experience some other type of emotional disruption before a test, they may end up performing poorly through no fault of their own. As noted previously in this book, negative emotional factors can be particularly consequential for students living in lower socioeconomic conditions. A student of mine who attempted to exit the class early during a history test summarized these stressors very candidly: "Mr. Dueck, my girlfriend and I broke up today, I got kicked out of my house last night, and after school I think I'm getting my ass kicked. Today is not a good day for me to take a test on World War II." To ignore these factors and insist that the student take the test regardless would be like asking a sprinter to perform despite a twisted ankle.

Outside factors can negatively affect typically high-performing students as well. A student-athlete just through a week of grueling volleyball playoff matches, or an academically motivated student facing multiple tests on the same date, could easily stumble on a test. A testing approach that insists on rigid time lines and forbids retests may reflect reality—just not the reality of what a student has truly learned.

Traditional Testing Approaches Discourage Mastery

For too much of my teaching career, I discouraged student mastery of learning—at least in the classroom. This was not true on the volleyball court. As a competitive coach, I approached our season of play with mastery as the ultimate goal. I had the team practice for hours each week, and I'd set up exhibition matches to hone their skills. After each game, I would highlight what we needed to practice to improve for the next game. I videotaped games so that we could examine the footage frame by frame to determine how to better spike the ball.

My colleague Chris Terris is both an English teacher and a basketball coach. He recently shared with me the following epiphany:

> It took me a long time to act more like a basketball coach in my English classroom. The tools I used for encouraging the passion and excellence in sport for my players were not the tools I transferred to the classroom for my students. Thankfully, I reached this epiphany moment before I reached the end of my career.

When it comes to classroom tests, we too often send the message to students that *they must get it right the first time.* If we reflect at all on the tested content, it is by telling frustrated students what they should have done once the testing is over. Yet in nearly every other area of the real world, we embrace and celebrate mastery through repeated effort. The underdog in the movie who tries and tries again despite overwhelming adversity inevitably triumphs in the end. In our own hobbies and passions, we reap emotional reward by repeatedly doing the same things and showing improvement, even if in the smallest of increments. Perhaps our students would learn better if we put systems in place to truly support and celebrate student mastery in the classroom.

Traditional Approaches Ignore the Learning That Occurs *During* Testing

We are wired to continue learning throughout our lives (Medina, 2008; Posner & Rothbart, 2000; Ratey, 2008). If learning is an active rather than a static process, there must be implications for the classroom. Teachers have organized learning and the measurement of learning into limited time frames for a long time; in fact, it could be said that our education system is built upon time restraints (Rshaid, 2011). Too often I was the dictator in the classroom who decided when learning qualified for measurement and when it didn't. For most of my career, I held the position that learning occurring *before* a unit test could be assessed, but learning that occurred *after* a test—even though I encouraged it—could not.

It is common for teachers to go over the correct test responses once the tests have been graded. Unfortunately, as Wiliam (2011) notes, "As soon as students get a grade, the learning stops" (p. 123). I used to go over nearly every test question after the fact, even though it was obvious that most students were tuning me out. If there is no opportunity for students to revisit the material, master it, and improve on their grades, we should expect such apathy. Students will not be interested in running to the wharf if it is clear to them that the ship has already sailed.

Potential Retesting Problems

Retesting is not without its own problems. Following are a few of the issues that educators may encounter when attempting to provide students with additional opportunities to master material.

Students May Need to Complete a Second Test in Its Entirety

Asking students to complete an entire second test can be discouraging for students. For those who are generally high-performing, problems on the first test are usually limited to a select few concepts, so redoing the whole test is a colossal waste of time. For students who are generally low-performing, particularly those living with chronic stress factors, the problems are more likely related to issues with concentration, memory, effort, and motivation (Erikson, Drevets, & Schulkin, 2003; Johnson, 1981; Lupien, King, Meaney, & McEwen, 2001). Years of academic struggles lead many of the latter students to dread testing situations, so asking them to redo a test on which they've already performed poorly is a recipe for blatant refusal. Students in the middle of the spectrum are often comfortable with a passing grade and may not see a benefit in repeating the entire test. In all cases, if you take an all-or-nothing approach to retesting, be prepared for most students to select "nothing."

Most teachers I know don't love spending every weekend grading stacks of tests so high as to allow them to relate with the climbers of Mt. Everest. Asking them to deliver an entire second test is like asking them to climb the mountain only to be buried in an avalanche. The amount of paperwork is tiring, cumbersome, and horribly inefficient. With many school districts reining in photocopier budgets, it is also increasingly unlikely that printing reams of retests is even an option.

Retests Take Up Valuable Class Time

In situations where students embrace full retests and teachers are eager to double their grading loads, completing the curriculum on time becomes an issue. Retests gobble up precious hours, so having students complete them during regular class can make it difficult for students to meet their learning targets for the year. In addition, students who are *not* taking the retests must find something to do with their time.

Retests Can Provide Data of Little Value

Of what value are retest data? Even if students do better on their retests than they did on their original tests, teachers may still not know whether their learning has truly improved. For instance, in the case of full retests, students who focus on studying the areas in which they made mistakes on the first test could score lower on the retests while actually doing better on the areas of concern. Alternatively, students could further improve on areas where they were already strong and thus receive a higher score on the retest without showing improvement in problem areas.

Retests May Not Reflect Authentic Learning

It is tempting for teachers who want to offer retests to simply readminister the first test without making any significant changes to it. These types of retests may not reflect authentic improvements in student learning, as students might memorize key questions from the first test in order to answer them correctly on the second attempt.

Strategies for Addressing Potential Retesting Problems

Here are some strategies for addressing the potential retesting problems outlined above.

Strategy #1: Offer Focused Revision and Customized Retests

STEP 1: Reorganize the test. It is nearly impossible to isolate learning outcomes when sections of a test consist of blended topics. For retests to be effective, they should be organized according to topic rather than format (e.g., multiple choice, short answer). As an example, consider a test that I designed on the Great Depression. I divided the test into the following sections and values:

1. The United States in the 1920s (11 points)
2. Causes of the Depression (4 points)
3. Roosevelt's efforts to end the Depression (5 points)
4. Reactions to Roosevelt's initiatives (7 points)
5. The end of the Depression (6 points)

On this test, both the format and point values of the questions varied within and across each section. For instance, the first section had eight multiple-choice questions and a question requiring a three-point-paragraph answer for a total of 11 points, whereas the third section asked for five definitions worth a point apiece. When designing each section on the original test, it is a good idea to also consider the corresponding section of a potential retest. When I was designing the test on the Great Depression, I created two sections for each topic—one for the original test and one for the retest—reflecting different question formats.

STEP 2: Create and distribute a tracking sheet. After students have completed the first test, grade it as you normally would. However, upon handing it back to your students, append a tracking sheet such as the one shown in Figure 4.1 for your students to fill out. The

Figure 4.1
Sample Tracking Sheet for Test

Name: _Jon Black_   Date: _April 3, 2010_

Topic	Value	Score	%	Retest? (✓)
The United States in the 1920s	11	8	73%	
Causes of the Depression	4	1	25%	
Roosevelt's efforts to end the Depression	5	1	20%	
Reactions to Roosevelt's New Deal	7	7	100%	
The end of the Depression	6	4	67%	
Total	33	23	70%	

Total points: _23_ out of 33   **Overall test score:** _70%_

UNIT TERMS:

☐ I DID complete all of the terms for this unit on either cards or sheets.

☑ I did NOT complete either the cards or the term list for this unit.

Reason: _I didn't think I needed to; I felt prepared._

PREPARATION:

What **overall grade** (percentage or letter) am I hoping to achieve in this course? _85%_

☐ I did all that I could to achieve my goal in preparing for this test.

☑ I can make the following adjustments to increase my grade:

✓ _complete all vocabulary cards_

✓ _make a practice quiz to test myself_

✓ _____

tracking sheet allows students to indicate whether or not they intend to retest any portion of the test and to supply information about their test-preparation and goal-setting skills. It also helps students create a graphic representation of their strengths and weaknesses in just a few minutes, thus actively involving them in the assessment process. After all the tracking sheets are completed and handed in, review them. Encourage students who request a retest to add different study routines to their sheets.

The data on your students' tracking sheets can help to inform conversations with them about their study habits. In some cases, it will be obvious to you when students need to better prepare for tests. When appropriate, you can even make the implementation of effective study routines a prerequisite for taking a retest. It is important to frame such prerequisites as supports for, rather than barriers to, retesting. Let your students know that they can expect a similar outcome on their retests if they don't make an effort to prepare effectively.

STEP 3: Help struggling learners to close the gap. Closely monitor the retesting decisions of your struggling learners. Such students will often choose to retest only one section of a test, and reluctantly at that. Putting in the effort to have struggling learners succeed on retests can fundamentally change their future learning assessment trajectory.

STEP 4: Track the improvement. You can track retesting data using a computer-based grading program. Consider the following example. The student in question—let's call him Bill—decided to retest the second and third sections of the Great Depression test. On the original test, he received a 1 out of 4 and a 1 out 5, respectively, on those sections; on his retest, he improved by 2 points on the second section and 3 points on the third. Here is the breakdown of Bill's scores on both tests, with his retest scores in parentheses next to the scores from the original test:

Section	Score (Retest Score)
The United States in the 1920s	8/11
Causes of the Depression	1/4 (3/4) + 2
Roosevelt's efforts to end the Depression	1/5 (4/5) + 3
Reactions to Roosevelt's initiatives	4/7
The end of the Depression	4/6
Total:	*18/33 (23/33) + 5*

According to the system I've devised, I enter a 1 in the first (tenths) decimal place in my grading program for students who show improvement on their retests, and the amount by which their scores have improved in the last two decimal places. Using this system, my entry for Bill would be 23.105—That is, an overall test score of 23, a 1 to indicate improvement on the retest, and 05 to indicate the degree by which Bill's score improved. (I don't worry about the effect that the .105 has on Bill's overall grade, but if I did I could easily create a second column without the decimals.)

Here are some reasons why this strategy is effective in ensuring that retests are successful:

1. Students take ownership of the process. Any teacher who has ever handed back a set of graded tests knows just how predictable students' reactions are. At first they appear to care about what you have to say; some even lean forward to savor your every word. Then, all of a sudden, they don't seem to care at all. Why the change? They've seen their grades, and now that's all they care about.

Unfortunately, schools have trained students to be grade-focused rather than learning-focused. As educators, we have placed incredible importance upon grades, and too often we have not allowed students to do anything to improve their results after they've been assessed. Why should students care about what they should have done on any given test if they aren't given the chance to revisit it? My retesting system addresses these issues. I have personally seen students in my class shift from apathetic to engaged when tests were returned to them. No longer mere bystanders to the assessment process, the students use their tracking sheets to determine areas of personal strengths and weaknesses. To a background din of fingers tapping on calculators, I've heard comments like, "Wow, I rocked that section!" and "Darn it, what a silly mistake, I'm going to retest that."

Perhaps the most powerful feature of my retesting system is the fact that it lets students determine which portions of their original test will function as formative assessments and which will remain summative. Allowing students to track their own learning invites them into a process that is far too often reserved for teachers alone. By ensuring that final grading takes place only after actual learning has occurred, we are adhering to the rule proposed by Alfie Kohn (1994): "Never grade students while they are still learning" (p. 41).

2. The resulting data are tangible. Students glean very important data from this retesting system. They can celebrate areas of strength and strategically focus on tackling concepts that they've not yet mastered. Teachers also benefit by obtaining feedback about their own performance through the testing process, especially when tests are subdivided by topic. For instance, if a particular section on a test receives a disproportionate number of wrong answers, the teacher can think back to when the topic was covered in class and try pinpointing what went wrong. Perhaps the teacher's instructional delivery was flawed, or there was a distraction in the school on the day that material was covered. Regardless of the reason, the teacher can decide to revisit that topic and perhaps adjust his or her instruction for more effective delivery.

Retesting data can also affect parent-teacher conversations. I'm guilty of using the time-honored trifecta of directives for student improvement when talking to parents: "Johnny should pay more attention in class, study more for tests, and complete all of his homework. Next!" Though these suggestions may be sound, they don't offer parents much in the area of new information. By contrast, retesting data can include the following tangible items:

- Original and retest scores
- Who is taking advantage of retests (and to what extent)
- The degree to which student results improved on retests
- The concepts students were able to master
- Areas students need to focus on further

Supplied with these data, teachers are able to give parents a more personalized account of their children's areas of strength and weakness and suggest adjustments to their study habits for greater success. If you are striving to develop a more personalized learning environment, the retesting system discussed here is incredibly valuable.

3. Students engage in focused readjustment of their learning routines. Learners benefit when they focus on specifics rather than the whole. As one of my homeschooling friends likes to say, "My children and I most enjoy learning when we go deep down the rabbit hole." Retesting—particularly when applied to struggling learners—is a far more inviting process when it is focused on the details. Here are some effective ways to ensure a focused retesting process:

- Offer study sessions that focus on only one or two key ideas. These sessions can be run during class, at lunchtime, or after school.
- Provide engaging extension activities that students may take home to reinforce topics covered in class.
- Make web-based tutorials available for students to watch repeatedly if necessary. One software application for doing this is Camtasia (www.techsmith.com/camtasia.html).
- Reassign homework that was incomplete or finished incorrectly.

4. Teachers grade smarter, not harder. Some sections of retests can literally be graded in the time it takes to pick up the paper from the student and walk back across the room. A retest section can be as simple as a few multiple-choice questions or a small diagram. In my experience, devoting the time I saved by not grading homework

In 2008 I was given a class of at-risk learners who were identified as having both academic and behavioral problems. Most of these students had failed previous social studies courses and seemed destined to fail mine, too. One student, Raymond, stood out immediately: he was friendly, he attended all his classes, he was relatively engaged in class, and he seemed to be trying hard. However, Raymond's academic confidence was very low. He had moved from school to school and he struggled to fit in socially. He spoke negatively about his abilities, and his negative self-image seemed to fuel his academic apathy. He confessed that in previous years he had studied very little and usually declined offers of support.

On our first unit test of the year, Raymond scored 42 percent. After completing his tracking sheet and determining his percentages on each section, he quietly approached my desk and asked if he could take his test home to show his mother. Because I don't want test questions passed among students from year to year, I have a firm policy of not allowing tests to leave my room unless they're in the hands of another teacher, so I said no. He then asked if he could have a copy of his completed tracking sheet. The photocopier was in the office near my classroom, so I quickly ducked out to copy his form. I was perplexed as to why he would want to show such a low score to his mom, so I asked him to explain.

"Well, look at it," he replied. "Look at the second section, on the stock market."

I looked, and there it was, like a flashing beacon: He had scored 2 out of 2. Given the structure of the tracking sheet, he had written his score for that section in the appropriate column: 100 percent.   *(cont.)*

to reassessing selected test sections results in a net *reduction* in the overall amount of grading. What's more, the resulting data are more accurate measures of student learning than are the nebulous data gleaned from graded homework.

5. Struggling learners benefit. According to Wiliam and Black (1998), struggling learners gain the most when teachers adopt formative assessment procedures. My experiences with retesting support this finding. There are at least four distinct benefits of the retesting system discussed here for at-risk learners:

1. When tests are subdivided by topic, students are able to begin by tackling those sections in which they feel most confident. Giving students the chance to start strong allows them to gain momentum as they move on to more challenging topics.
2. Many researchers now believe that academic competency is a reflection of how effectively our brains combine disparate information into a coherent product (Medina, 2008). If this is true, we can assume that chunking questions together by topic increases the likelihood of such coherence developing.
3. The availability of a second chance gives students hope. One year, following the first test of the year, I asked students a few questions about their test-taking experience. As you can see from the responses in Figure 4.2, knowing that a retesting "lifeline" was present made a difference.

4. Subdividing tests by topic allows students to experience micro-successes in certain areas and enjoy grades usually reserved for "the smart kids." This allows students with low self-esteem to develop what Dweck (2006) refers to as a growth mind-set. The belief that improvement—a pillar of the growth mind-set—is possible is critical if students are to try again in the face of failure.

6. Issues unrelated to content knowledge can be identified. It's possible for students to improve on one section of a retest without having revised their study habits. Although this could be the result of a sudden epiphany, other factors are more likely. For example, it could be that the improvement is due to changes in the question format between the original test and the retest. Research shows that students with reading difficulties struggle with multiple-choice questions (Cassels & Johnstone, 1984). Many such learners are quick to embrace diagram questions but shy away from questions that involve written responses. This being the case, I have sought to provide a balanced selection of question formats on tests to address different learning styles. I have adjusted many questions to read as follows: "Using sentences or a combination of drawing and written descriptions, indicate . . . ."

Improvements on retests could also be due to social-emotional factors. We know that many of our students arrive at school each day carrying the incredible weight of challenges related to poverty, for instance, which can greatly affect their ability

---

PERSONAL STORY CONTINUED

"My mom and I are used to seeing 42 percent," he said, "but never in my life has my name been on a sheet of paper with 100 percent on it."

Before I could respond, he continued: "This would make a difference for me at home." Raymond's last comment hit me like a ton of bricks. Not wanting to pry, I didn't ask him how the tracking sheet would make a difference for him at home.

In the weeks following the test, Raymond's behavior changed to such an extent that it shocked his learning-assistance teacher, Cindy Postlethwaite. One afternoon, she blasted into my room asking what the heck had happened to Raymond—not only had he dramatically improved his support-block attendance, but he was also completing his homework and studying diligently for the next unit test. Most perplexing of all, he was gloating to anyone who would listen that he'd "scored 100 percent in social studies." As his learning-assistance teacher put it, "When you work with at-risk students, it is a nice change to have to rein in overconfidence!"

For the record, Raymond never scored lower than 55 percent on any of his unit tests for the remainder of the year. His use of better study skills, focused revision, and retesting resulted in a final course standing of 62 percent, and he passed the standardized provincial exam at the end of the year.

Figure 4.2
Student Feedback on Retesting

---

5. **Did it make a difference to you knowing that you could rewrite sections where you did not do so well?** ■ yes   ☐ no

Explain because its easier then doing the hole test

---

5. **Did it make a difference to you knowing that you could rewrite sections where you did not do so well?** ☑ yes   ☐ no

Explain I Did really bad on the essay and would like to rerwite it porobally

---

5. **Did it make a difference to you knowing that you could rewrite sections where you did not do so well?** ☑ yes   ☐ no

Explain That if you do bad on one section you cand redeve it so I felt more cofendent

---

to do well academically, particularly on tests (Jensen, 2013). Likewise, students navigating the complex world of relationships may not place doing well on a test as their top priority. Allowing students two separate chances to display their knowledge will help to reduce the effect of nonacademic issues on assessment data.

7. Learners at all points on the spectrum benefit. Although I have seen my retesting system benefit struggling learners the most, the students most *interested* in using the system have been those with the strongest performance records—that is, those who are competing for university scholarships and academic awards. Such students typically face a lot of pressure to do as well as possible on their tests, and tend to have heavy course loads as well as extracurricular responsibilities. For these students, coming in at lunchtime or after school to improve on a test section makes sense. However, designing retests that suit the narrow needs of top students can be frustrating for teachers. In certain cases, I have taken the time to creatively customize the retesting experience for exceptional learners (see sidebar).

8. Conflicts over grading decisions can be lessened. Some test questions can be worded in such a way as to invite multiple interpretations. Retesting students on the learning target addressed by a vaguely worded question allows them to prove their understanding of the material.

9. There is less temptation to cheat. When tests are one-time-only events, the pressure to excel may tempt students to do so by whatever means possible. As my colleague Chris Terris notes, "Using a retesting system lowers the temptation for my students to cheat. If they know there is another chance, they will try their best, take risks, and later on, they will have the opportunity to revisit errors they make during the test." Building learning environments that are flexible and accommodating can

---

PERSONAL STORY

Sam was one of my top students in 12th grade history, consistently scoring in the 98–100 percent range on both tests and assignments. One day, he made a simple multiple-choice error on a test, and before I'd even had time to grade it, he approached me to ask about a retest.

"Mr. Dueck," he said, "I made the mistake of indicating that Britain controlled Syria after World War I, but I now know it was France. I know everything else about the topic of mandates, so no matter how you ask the question, my retest will be successful. Can I just have the retest right now and score my inevitable 100 percent?"

I took one look at Sam and knew that I would need to come up with a retest that would further his learning, challenge his abilities, and—on account of his smugness—be a little entertaining as well. I told him that his retest would be unique: he would be required to conduct research on World War I mandates and discover something that I did not know and that I would find intriguing. He would need to let me know when he was ready to report his findings, but I would choose the time and place.

Though Sam found the conditions of his retest a little weird, he grinned in anticipation of the challenge. About three days later, he arrived to class early and enthusiastically declared that he had discovered a very interesting tidbit about the World War I mandates. He was sure that I was unaware of this historical wonder or else I would have mentioned it in class. As he was about to share his finding with me, I reminded him that it was up to me to choose the time and place for the retest.

A week or so later, I was driving home when I happened to pass by the hardware store where Sam worked. I needed to *(cont.)*

---

pick up a few light bulbs, so I popped in and noticed that Sam was restocking the shelves.

I suddenly realized that the retesting opportunity had arrived.

"Now?!" exclaimed Sam, setting down a box of nails.

"What better time and place?" I responded.

Sam proceeded to explain to me the system of Class C mandates determined by the League of Nations after World War I. I was both surprised and intrigued, and awarded Sam a perfect grade for his efforts. (Indeed, I suggest that anyone interested in post-1919 African politics look up Class C mandates.)

As this story shows, retesting can allow the most gifted and hard-working students to refine the components of their testing experience while also improving student-teacher relationships.

send students the message that authentic understanding is the best avenue to good grades.

Strategy #2: The "Double-Dip" System for Quizzes

If your retesting system becomes popular among students, they will probably start asking for it to be applied to quizzes as well. When my students initially did so, I was horrified—I felt like I had enough on my plate designing retests, and didn't feel that I had the time or energy to go down that road. Still, a re-quiz system made sense: as students prepare for their final unit tests, their ability to better perform on assessments for each particular topic also tend to improve. Some students find that they understand individual topics better as the pieces of the whole unit fall into place. If quizzes affect students' overall grades, then it's only logical that they'd want the opportunity to redo them if they perform poorly. So I understood why students wanted re-quizzes, but I also knew that it would be a lot of work to design, administer, and grade them.

One day, a very capable student of mine asked to take a re-quiz. I was very busy at that moment as it was the day before a major unit test, and I felt that I did not have one minute to spare. I was conflicted: though I had told myself that I was to accurately reflect student competency according to prescribed learning outcomes, I had thus far been avoiding the re-quiz dilemma—yet it was obvious that quizzes, which occurred early in the unit, no longer reflected students' true understanding of the material.

At the spur of the moment, I came up with a solution. I told my student to take the unit test the following day as scheduled, and that I would adjust her quiz score to reflect the score she received on the corresponding section of the test. In that moment, the double-dip system was born.

This system requires that teachers design each quiz so that its value matches that of the corresponding section on the unit test. For example, if a teacher knows that one section on an upcoming English test will focus on nouns and have a value of 4 points, he or she might create a quiz on nouns with a value of 4 points (or a multiple of 4). Under this system, each section of a test counts not only as part of the test itself, but also as a re-quiz of a prior assessment.

The double-dip re-quiz system is effective for the following reasons:

1. It saves students time. A large number of tests and retests can overwhelm students. At times it might be appropriate to encourage students not to take advantage of retesting, especially if the potential benefit is small relative to the amount of extra time the student must invest in the process. Some students are barely able to stay afloat with their regular course requirements as it is. I have seen a student spend so much time preparing for a retest that he ended up missing out on the learning taking place in the unit. The double-dip re-quiz system allows students to make one concerted effort to study and essentially retake the unit quizzes at the same time as they take the unit test; in other words, this system allows students to study smarter, not harder.

2. It saves the teacher time. It seemed to me that constructing and administering re-quizzes was a waste of time because it *was* a waste of time. Why create re-quizzes when, if carefully designed, each section of the unit test can function as such on its own?

3. It offers just enough incentive for some reluctant students to prepare better for their unit tests. You can impress upon students who have not performed well on earlier quizzes that a little more effort might pay large dividends. Consider using the following formulations:

- "I want to measure your *current* understanding, not what you used to know."
- "Many of you have been studying for the upcoming test. Congratulations! You will be able to replace your old quiz scores with better results."
- "Remember that quiz we had two weeks ago? You should know much more about that topic now. During tomorrow's test you will have the opportunity to get in a time machine and take that quiz again."

4. It allows the original quizzes to serve as formative assessments. Quizzes taken during the course of a unit can provide very valuable data even if the grades are eventually replaced by those on the corresponding unit-test sections. Students who score poorly on quizzes can revisit the quiz topics and improve their understanding. Used in this manner, quizzes are excellent formative assessments. When preparing students for summative assessments, the administering of frequent, smaller assessments has been proven to be more effective than simply studying (Pyc & Rawson, 2010). Treating the results from quizzes as evidence of practice can guide students to a better understanding of the material. The double-dip re-quiz system makes the distinction between summative and formative assessments clear for everyone.

Conclusion

Since introducing retesting to my classroom, I have only had one student oppose the system, and the circumstances serve to illustrate an important point. I had recently decided to adopt retests in my 12th grade history class and was explaining the specifics to my students when a very capable student, Rafael, raised his hand to ask a question.

"So, if I score a 97 percent on a test, I can take a retest?" he asked.

"Yes," I replied, wondering if I had properly described the system.

"And I don't have to take the whole test over again?"

"No," I responded, "only the section or sections that you choose to retest."

"I don't like it," said Rafael emphatically. I was not the only person taken aback; Rafael's classmates turned to look at him. "I don't like this system at all," he concluded.

"What don't you like?" I asked.

"You know why students will do this, Mr. Dueck," he replied. "They want to do better. Students will take these retests because they want to do better. Students should have to do the whole test over again if they want to improve. I mean, I always thought retests were a form of punishment."

With this last statement, it became clear to me what Rafael's problem with my retesting policy was. Rafael was a student who enjoyed all the benefits of the regular schooling system; he played by the rules, academics came easily to him, and he didn't welcome any system that might help other students close the gap.

As I was gathering my thoughts to respond, one of Rafael's classmates, Kim, raised her hand. With defiance in her voice, she spoke of her job at a local restaurant.

"You know, Rafael, at my job, I'm trained to seat families, understand the menu, serve tables, and operate the cash register. I'm tested on each of these elements. The funny thing is, once I've passed a test on one element, I'm not tested on it again. I just need to focus on the things that I don't know. But I would not expect you to know that, because you don't have a real job."

I asked Kim to tone it down a little, but I could empathize with her general sentiment. Rafael came from a fairly wealthy family, he had an older sibling at a prestigious university, and he was a regular contender for academic awards. In that moment, it dawned on me: the lords of academia do not wish to share power with the peasants. Kim knew it, too.

I have shared my retesting system with educators around the world, and it turns out that Rafael is not alone. Tensions arise whenever we make changes that reduce the academic disparity among students. Those who have benefitted from the more traditional, regimented forms of testing may feel that their hierarchy is threatened as less successful students gain access to academic proficiency. Retesting may require a community to embrace a cultural paradigm shift. If one of the central purposes of the school system has been to sort and rank students, a retesting will be seen as a challenge.

Opposition to retesting can be taken as proof that a change is long overdue. For too long, we have maintained a status quo that increases the achievement gap in schools, even when we *know* that not all students receive the same level of support. Generations of teachers have taken it for granted that some students will fail, a select few will rise to the very top, and the remainder will fall somewhere in the middle. This is a predictable outcome of rigid testing procedures. If learning is the ultimate goal, we should allow for the possibility that *every* student can fully meet prescribed learning outcomes, and that this should be celebrated rather than scorned. In too many schools, the industrial model of education is alive and well, and the opponents of retesting cling to it. Perhaps it is time to recognize that the bell curve is so cracked and outdated that it too belongs in a museum.

Retesting has become a cornerstone of my teaching experience. I believe that I am reflecting the real world when I offer students a second chance to demonstrate capacity. The top students are still receiving the bulk of the academic awards, but the achievement gap is shrinking. Retesting finally allows both teachers and learners to make learning the fixed standard and time the variable.

Relationships improve when more students have the opportunity to succeed. Parents and students have meaningful conversations about changing study habits to improve results. Teachers have more positive relationships with their students when they become advocates rather than the adversaries. Most importantly, students shift their self-concepts of themselves as learners.

Frequently Asked Questions

Q: Do you have prerequisites for students who ask for retests?

A: Retests are not a right. Students should not come to demand or expect retests regardless of their conduct or approach to learning. It is reasonable to ask that students complete their homework or attend a study session before being eligible for a retest. Some teachers are tempted to make these requirements quite daunting; whatever requirements you decide to put in place should *support learning* rather than simply deterring student access to retests.

Q: Do some students fail to prepare for the first test, knowing that they can just get a retest? If so, what can be done to avoid this situation?

A: I have seldom encountered this problem personally, but I've been asked the question enough times to know that it's a concern. Students who work to the best of their ability will perform as well as can be expected. If you develop a culture of effort that promotes study, student preparation will not be thwarted. Offering retests is a way to send the message that the achievement of understanding is more important than *when* the understanding occurs.

Still, despite our best intentions, some students might see the retesting system as giving them an opportunity to "kick the tires" during an initial test, thinking that they'll automatically get a chance for a redo. Here are some strategies for dealing with such situations:

- Encourage students to do as well as possible on the initial test by letting them know that this will reduce the effort they might have to put into a retest later.
- Make the initial test format more user-friendly than that of the retest, such as by offering more choices on it. Since adopting this practice myself, I have noticed that fewer students call in

sick on the day of the initial test. At the same time, be sure not to make the retest so difficult that it deters students who want a reassessment. A slight change in format between the initial test and the retest can separate those students who are serious about retesting from those seeking an easy way out.

- Blend the initial and retest scores. For example, one of my colleagues employs a system that calls for the final score to be a sum of 25 percent of the lower score and 75 percent of the higher.
- Consider the initial test and the retest to be natural parts of your assessment system regardless of how they are used. Some students will inevitably fail to study for the initial test—this is predictable. Others will do well on certain sections despite their lack of preparation and then decide to reassess the sections on which they performed poorly. Is this a bad use of the system? Perhaps it's strategic on the part of the student, though it taxes the teacher's time.
- If a pattern emerges of students not being prepared for the initial test, consider using quizzes as prerequisites for tests. Poor quiz scores might identify those students who are not studying or who are fundamentally unprepared. Quizzes consisting of a few of the more difficult questions can raise red flags and indicate the need for interventions.

Q: If retests are held during class, what do you do for those students who do not retest at all, or who retest only a section or two?

A: This dilemma can be transformed into an opportunity for personalized learning. Allow students who are not retesting or whose retests are very short to engage in meaningful learning activities while their classmates retest. Students can use this time to complete homework from other courses, read, enjoy extension activities, or work on long-term projects. I would not recommend using this time to start the next unit in the course, as the students most likely to benefit from the introduction are likely to be completing retests at that time.

Q: Do some students do worse on a retest than on the initial test? If so, what can be done about this?

A: Some students do worse on retests. There are different possible reasons for this, each with a different possible solution:

- *Misplaced confidence.* Students who choose not to prepare prior to the retest may do so out of a false sense of readiness, thinking that reviewing the material by taking the initial test is sufficient preparation. Encourage these students not only to study prior to the retest, but to employ different study routines than they did before the initial test.
- *Heavy workload.* Some students simply get overwhelmed trying to keep track of their upcoming assessments, let alone doing well on them. Taking part in the retesting system may actually hamper such students. Spending too much time trying to increase their scores on retests might keep them from learning the current material, which in turn may result in them needing retests later on—the cycle can be endless. Students who have trouble keeping up with the learning schedule should be encouraged not to retest or to retest only small amounts.
- *Inadequate study skills.* Students who appear to be studying hard for a retest only to do worse on it than on the initial test should be shown more effective study routines.

Q: When a student does worse on the retest than on the initial test, which score do you record?

A: I keep the higher of the two scores for the following reasons:

- Perhaps the student is better equipped to do well using the format of the test that resulted in the higher score.

- The student may have been affected by negative factors unrelated to the course on the day that he or she achieved the lower score.
- In my provincial jurisdiction, the Ministry of Education records the higher of the two scores regardless of the order in which they were administered.

More important than which score to report is figuring out why the student's progress may have regressed. A student who performs poorly on a retest is a learner who needs more attention and support. You should be concerned if a student receives the disappointment of a poor result on a retest. If this occurs, discussing study routines and the possibility of test anxiety with the student can be helpful.

Q: Do you administer retests at lunchtime?

A: I have. If the lunch session is too short for an entire retest, I have had students complete sections of the retest at subsequent lunchtimes. For example, if the retest consists of eight sections, I might administer sections 1–4 on Monday at lunch and sections 5–8 on Tuesday at the same time.

Q: Since adopting retests, do you have more difficulty completing the curriculum on time?

A: No, but I did have to make some adjustments. I used to need all the class time available in order to plow through the required content, and even then I would often fall short as the year or semester drew to a close. At about the same time I introduced retests, I reconfigured my content delivery to involve fewer lectures; I felt that my students were simply spending too much time mindlessly taking notes. I replaced the traditional note-taking sessions with more videos and discussion and provided students with note outlines that corresponded to the various media I brought to class. These outlines required much less time for students to complete, as they only needed to insert main ideas and interesting details. The result was a more efficient use of class time and more time for more meaningful learning opportunities.

Q: What do you do if a student claims not to be ready to take the test?

A: It depends on the specific situation and on the students involved. Here are two scenarios I have frequently encountered:

- *The student is probably ready, but nervous.* In this scenario, encourage the student to take the test as scheduled and remind him or her of the availability of a retest in order to lower his or her anxiety. Consider saying, "You always have the retest to rely on, so why not take the test and see how you do? This way we can at least narrow down the topics you need to focus on more."
- *The student isn't ready, but is willing to take the test.* In this scenario, it might be a waste of everyone's time and energy to administer the test. As my colleague Chris Terris puts it, "What kind of coach hopes to build up the confidence of players by putting them into a game when they're clearly unprepared? If we truly want to encourage the love of learning, embarrassing someone does not seem like a good idea." I tend to agree with Chris. While other students are taking the test, use the time to better prepare the unprepared student.

5

CREATIVITY

Creativity is as important in education as literacy,
and we should treat it with the same status.

—*Ken Robinson*

It is the supreme art of the teacher to awaken
joy in creative expression and knowledge.

—*Albert Einstein*

I have found that creativity and engagement are the two factors that most determine the quality of student assignments and test responses. The extent to which students demonstrate these attributes depends largely on the opportunities available to them (Brownlie & King, 2011).

I was encouraged to embrace more creativity in my classroom by a strong dose of interdepartmental competition. When a new 12th grade English literature teacher, Ms. Searcy, first arrived at our high school and started to use unconventional teaching strategies, I was one of the many teachers who initially treated her approach as a mere novelty. My reluctance to investigate any further began to evaporate as I noticed how excited my students were about Ms. Searcy's class. Her approach was far from conventional: she had her students write on the windows with markers, brought dramatic props to class, and held puppet shows. One time she even decorated the school sports bus for a visit to a rival high school, which she termed a "a trip to hell"—not only as a way to engage the students, but also to connect the trip to her class's reading of John Milton's *Paradise Lost*.

It was obvious that my students were becoming more interested in Ms. Searcy's class than in mine, so I decided to strike back. My futile attempt involved the use of friendly banter incorporating historical themes. I soon decided to declare war on English lit. I'd visit Ms. Searcy's class and scowl. I took to substituting the names of aggressor nations in my history class with the term "English lit." I would stand outside the door of Ms. Searcy's class and lobby students not to attend. Ms. Searcy's class returned fire: one evening, her students "decorated" my classroom with a few thousand sticky notes that had sonnets written on them. To this day, I will occasionally open a history book to find a neon-pink sonnet staring back at me.

Admittedly, I taught history in a very teacher-centered manner. Though I believed that my approach was interesting and reflected my passion for history, I assumed that I, as the teacher, was the gatekeeper of the learning portal. Many students appeared to truly enjoy my course, but I began to recognize that there remained room to dig deeper into true student creativity, engagement, and passion for learning. In hindsight, perhaps I was too often the only person in class truly engaged in my lectures.

One day, I saw Ms. Searcy show a group of colleagues one of her students' assignments—a musical interpretation of a Robert Browning poem. The song was entertaining and insightful, and Ms. Searcy explained how it had fulfilled prescribed requirements. When another teacher asked how she intended to grade a song, she made the point that she didn't have to be a music teacher to know what learning targets to assess.

Creativity, Engagement, and Motivation

Creativity generally refers to a richness of ideas and originality of thinking, and we need more of it in the classroom (Pink, 2009). According to Ken Robinson (2001, 2009), creativity is going to be required by future generations to solve both current problems and those yet unseen. Putting students through the same educational regimens of generations past will not set them up for success in a world that rewards the unique. Robinson champions the notion of teaching *for* creativity by allowing students to pursue original thinking, innovation, and inquiry-based learning (2009). Daniel Pink (2009) makes a strong case that schools should abandon the traditional carrot-and-stick approach, arguing that learning and mastery occur much more readily in environments that promote autonomy through self-direction and purpose. However, creativity shouldn't be incorporated simply for the sake of variety; Beghetto and Kaufman (2013) point to evidence showing that it must be task appropriate in order to be effective. Medina (2008) makes the case for creativity as a tool for aiding understanding:

> Some schools and workplaces emphasize a stable rote-learned database. They ignore the improvisatory instincts drilled into us for millions of years. Creativity suffers. Others emphasize creative usage of a database, without installing a fund of knowledge in the first place. They ignore our need to obtain a deep understanding of a subject, which includes memorizing and storing a richly structured database. You get people who are great improvisers but don't have a depth of knowledge. (p. 38)

Learning is greatly enhanced through individual creativity, owner-ship, and empowerment. When learners are given the opportunity to explain and reason using their own creative skills, they are better able to demonstrate evidence of learning. If students in classrooms charac-terized by rote learning are prone to developing what Pace and Hem-mings (2007) call "an oppositional stance to schooling" (p. 17), we might assume the contrary to be true as well.

Engagement is the key to unlocking the intrinsic motivation to learn. Clearly, people are more engaged when tasks interest them. If you wish to have a compelling conversation with the stranger next to you on a plane, ask one simple question—"Do you have a hobby or passion?"—and expect to be amazed. This simple conversation-starter has introduced me to a young woman who was working on a science fiction movie script, a middle-aged man who collected Civil War uniforms, a teenager who was into shortwave radios, and a guy who collected steering wheels. Each of these people took great pleasure in dragging me down their respective rabbit holes, and personalized learning poured out of every account. People do not need to memorize the details of their hobbies, and why should they? As Medina (2008) notes, "We remember things better the more we elaborately encode the encounter, especially if we personalize it" (p. 111). Allowing students to be creative in the classroom is a way of personalizing learning (Rob-inson, 2001, 2009).

The human condition is based on connection and socialization. As a species, we've been storytellers since long before the advent of the written word. We draw meaning from interaction more so than from homework or lectures (Geary, 2011). Research confirms that when people are spurred on by curiosity, they learn more (Engel, 2013), and when intrigue and surprise are added to the mix, they remember more (Engel, 2013; Garner, Brown, Sanders, & Menke, 1992).

Given that we thrive on interaction and investigation, it should not be surprising that project-based activities enhance learning. Larmer and Mergendoller (2012) make the point that project-based learning blends many of the skills that teachers wish to encourage in isolation, including organization, the use of visual aids, and public speaking. Brooks and Dietz (2012) put it well:

> Good teachers set up classrooms rich in opportunities for students to construct integrated knowledge transferable across disciplines. They offer interdisciplinary, authentic investigations that provoke students to confront cognitive challenges in the pursuit of answers to their own questions. They invite students to think about ideas that matter to them and to resolve potential contradictions, and they help students to develop the skills and dispositions to think about those ideas at increasingly deep levels. (p. 65)

Some experts believe that state assessments are too narrow and do not adequately assess the multidimensional aspect of more complex learning activities (Doorey, 2012). Classroom instruction is too often guided by these rigid assessments (Rshaid, 2011). There is an argument to be made that broadening our approach to education will benefit all learners. As Robinson (2009) notes,

> The current system . . . puts severe limits on how teachers teach and students learn. Academic ability is very important, but so are other ways of thinking. People who think visually might love a particular topic or subject, but won't realize it if their teachers only present it in one, non-visual way. Yet our education systems increasingly encourage teachers to teach students in a uniform fashion. (p. 37)

Potential Problems with Creativity

As valuable as creativity is, there can be barriers to embracing its use in the classroom. Many teachers lament the fact that they are not using more innovation and exploration, often due to the following reasons.

1. Creativity is unpredictable. Traditional, paper-and-pen-based assessments are safe and familiar. Opening the door to more creative avenues can make teachers feel as though their control of the classroom will be compromised. Creative people possess a deep, broad, and flexible awareness of themselves that can fly in the face of conventional classroom norms. The very nature of people who color outside the lines will threaten those who cling to the belief that classrooms should be quiet and orderly. Highly creative people thrive on disorder, contradiction, and imbalance (*Encyclopedia Britannica,* 2014). Is there a more terrifying trifecta for a teacher attempting to manage a classroom? And if teachers themselves have even the tiniest flicker of creative interest, it is too often extinguished by the prevailing winds of familiarity, normalcy, and repetition.

2. Creativity can distract from prescribed learning outcomes. If a teacher rooted in tradition does have the courage to wander into the realm of the unknown, a single set of catastrophic results can forever convince him or her that the journey is not worth it. I can vividly remember being very excited to unveil what I thought was a cool puppet-show project idea, only to find that the students spent all their time designing puppet costumes and little or none on actual learning. Intricate puppet costumes might be linked to learning outcomes in textiles class, but they're unlikely to prepare students for a social studies final exam. Though creative projects can engage students, they can also waste valuable class time. Once the dust settles on a floor littered with art supplies, a teacher can be left with the realization that he or she will need to reteach the unit.

3. Creativity can lead to inflated grades for more artistically minded students. When students spend a large amount of time and effort on perfecting the aesthetics of a project, teachers are often tempted to reward them through grading. After a while, students can come to equate grades given for time, effort, and aesthetic results with those based on an understanding of the concepts being taught (O'Connor, 2010). When these students face standardized exams or unit tests, they may find themselves floundering.

4. Creativity can lead to deflated grades for at-risk students. Students who don't have the tools or opportunities to produce elegantly designed projects can be disadvantaged when it comes to visually creative assignments. A student with a keen understanding of the solar system may not have the materials at his or her disposal to construct a 3-D model or the structured and safe home environment in which to work on it.

5. The search for resources can become anarchic. Creative projects can often require resources outside the classroom. As I began allowing my students more creative avenues for demonstrating learning, they increasingly required such resources as cameras, thread, glue, costumes, and props that I didn't keep stocked in my class. When I would allow students to leave the classroom in search of these resources, I felt a loss of control. If my high school were to slide into a state of anarchy, I wouldn't be surprised if it were due to educators like me letting legions of students wander the hallways. Teachers who are willing to expand the learning environment outside the walls of the classroom might feel pressured by more traditionally minded colleagues to keep the halls and courtyards vacant and quiet.

6. Levels of creativity are difficult to assess. Imagine you've assigned a project to a group of students and encouraged them to approach it creatively. When the time comes to assess the students' projects, you find that they exhibit varying degrees of creativity. Moreover, you are tasked with grading according to a set of prescribed learning outcomes that don't stipulate creativity as a criterion. Beghetto and Kaufman (2013) point to the problem with this type of assessment when they ask, "How can something be original and at the same time conform to a set of task requirements?" (p. 12). What if two projects meet the basic learning targets, but one clearly exhibits far more creativity than the other? I refer to this dilemma as the "cutting board versus bookshelf" problem. Consider a woodshop assignment for which one student delivers a uniform chunk of finished wood and another hands in an ultra-contemporary bookshelf in the shape of a reading chair. Both students have technically met the criteria for the assignment, but one has displayed far more creativity and hard work than the other. What is the woodshop teacher to do in this case? He might stop requesting creativity altogether and start assigning the same simple birdhouse project to all students. All hail uniformity and tradition!

Strategies for Grading Creative Projects

Given these potential issues, it's not hard to see why so many teachers avoid assigning creative projects altogether. Conventional classroom assignments constitute the safest route, but unfortunately not the most productive one—and certainly not the most engaging one. It's possible that teachers will only come to embrace creativity when they feel empowered to assess it. This can actually have benefits for classroom management, as engaged students are focused students. When students feel a sense of purpose and are allowed free rein to explore what they're learning, concerns about fomenting anarchic conditions evaporate. Teachers just need to learn how best to quantify the unconventional.

Strategy #1: Major Project Planning Sheet

Before students start a project, be sure that they're aware of the targeted learning outcomes. One way to do this is by creating and distributing a Project Planning Sheet (see Figure 5.1). It's critical that students not lose sight of learning targets in the process of indulging their creativity. Too often, students are encouraged to focus on the project itself rather than on the learning outcomes that lie at the heart of it.

My Project Planning Sheet originated with one developed by Ms. Searcy, the English literature teacher. She used a template with two columns, one showing the learning outcomes to be addressed and the other showing how those learning outcomes are to be demonstrated. Ms. Searcy's template was designed to facilitate a conversation between the teacher and the student concerning a proposed project. When I first attempted to modify the template to address written proposals, I noticed that some struggling learners found it hard to identify the learning outcomes and link them to their project elements.

Figure 5.1
Project Planning Sheet

Name: _____ Date: _____

Focus: _____ Medium/Delivery: _____

What I am learning . . .	How I will show I have learned it . . .	
Learning Outcome	**Medium/Method**	**Details and/or Elements Covered**
☐ Compare the nature of **democratic** and **totalitarian** states & their impact on individuals.		

☐ Explain the rise to power of Hitler and National Socialism with reference to
  ☐ conditions that generated support for Nazism.
  ☐ Hitler's actions and policies.		

☐ Identify the **causes** of the **outbreak** of World War II in Europe and the Pacific.		

☐ Explain the **significance** of **key military events** in World War II, including
  ☐ BATTLE OF BRITAIN.
  ☐ attack on PEARL HARBOR.
  ☐ EL ALAMEIN.
  ☐ BATTLE OF MIDWAY.
  ☐ BATTLE OF STALINGRAD.
  ☐ NORMANDY LANDINGS.
  ☐ bombing of HIROSHIMA.		

☐ Explain how World War II **resulted in a realignment** of world power.		
☐ Describe the **impact** of **"total war."**		
☐ Describe the significance of **technology** developed prior to and during World War II.		
☐ Assess the impact of **mass communications** on political and military events prior to and during World War II.		
☐ Evaluate the **historical significance** of the HOLOCAUST.		

Additionally, many students found the amount of writing involved in completing the template to be a barrier. To address these concerns, I designed the revised Project Planning Sheet shown in Figure 5.1, which requires teachers to list all of the learning targets for the students beforehand. (As a general rule, for units with more than five learning targets, I often ask students to incorporate at least three in a project.) In the central column of the Project Planning Sheet, students are given the chance to explain how they might use different types of media to meet different targets. This planning step is of great benefit to students as it allows them to plan for maximum effectiveness. The third column requires students to list key details and elements of the project, including specific facts, sources, and arguments that demonstrate their understanding of the topic in a meaningful way. After all, an effective project doesn't skirt the edges of understanding, but rather dives into the center of it.

The Project Planning Sheet helps teachers to assess students' projects according to the prescribed learning outcomes. At this stage, for most classes outside of those devoted to art, it ought to be irrelevant whether a student performed a puppet show using Popsicle sticks or professional-looking marionettes; what matters is that he or she was able to effectively convey an understanding of the topic.

Here are some reasons why this strategy is effective:

1. The students and the teacher are all aware of the learning targets before the project starts. The prescribed learning outcomes are clearly listed on the Project Planning Sheet, and the checkbox beside each one ensures accountability. I recommend holding a short conference with each student before he or she embarks on the project to ensure that the planned project aligns with the course objectives and is personally meaningful to the student. The Project Planning Sheet can form the basis of this conversation and sustain the student's focus on the learning objectives once the project begins.

2. Prescribed learning outcomes form the foundation of the project. By ensuring that the project is based on prescribed learning

Janet was in 10th grade and was struggling academically. She had performed relatively well through middle school, but in the 9th grade her grades began to slide. Her middle school report cards indicated that she did well on projects and assignments but struggled in testing situations. A few of the comments on her report cards suggested that she experienced test anxiety and should be offered support in those situations.

It was clear that Janet worked very hard on making things look good and completed all her homework assignments. However, in high school, her courses offered fewer projects and more tests—and what few projects she did encounter were firmly rooted in the courses' learning objectives. Janet needed help focusing more on understanding these objectives. She had narrowly passed her previous grades by relying on hard work and designing attractive projects. The buffers she had previously enjoyed were no longer available.

outcomes, students can avoid the common trap of getting distracted by the process. If a student creates a wooden seesaw to demonstrate learning related to the concept of leverage in math class, the Project Planning Sheet should remind him that it is his understanding of the concept, not his woodworking skills, that matters.

3. Students are given the green light to have fun, explore, and invent. Amazing things can happen when students are encouraged to blend personal interests with school projects. The classroom can buzz with activity without you feeling as though you're about to lose control. I have seen projects as diverse as clay crematoriums and children's pop-up books devised to meet learning targets related to World War II. It's fun for students to take risks with challenging media. Teachers who are concerned that writing will fade into extinction need not worry: I have found that students who are engaged in the learning process will be far more likely to write than those who are apathetic. In my experience, once students are hooked on a project, the challenge is to limit the amount of writing they're willing to submit!

4. Teachers can grade smarter, not harder. The Project Planning Sheet makes grading exciting and enjoyable, as well as effective, by serving as a roadmap for each project. In addition, students themselves are active participants in the grading by checking off the learning targets met. What's more, rather than grading piles of virtually identical assignments, teachers can expect to face projects that are unique, refreshing, and innovative.

Strategy #2: Recognizing Creativity Without Using Grades

I learned early on that there should be a single set of learning targets for all students in a class. Unless the use of creativity is in and of itself a learning target, which is usually unlikely, meeting these targets in a noncreative way should not result in lowered grades, just as heightened levels of creativity should not be rewarded with higher grades. With this standard in place, the question remains: how should teachers recognize exceptionally creative projects?

At the outset of a project, students should be informed that they will all be graded according to the same standard—the extent to which they meet the learning targets. You may wish to recognize students who go beyond this standard, but it's best not to do so through grades. I believe it's better to recognize exceptional creativity by way of supplementary comments, school and classroom displays, phone calls to parents, mentions in school newsletters, Student of the Month recognition, and any other avenues that aren't reflected in the grade book. If we wish to encourage exploration, ingenuity, and passion, it is essential that we not pay for them using grades as the currency. As Pink (2009) points out, extrinsic rewards serve only to "crush creativity" (p. 57).

Here are some reasons why this strategy is effective:

1. All students are held to the same standard. A very basic project that fully meets the learning targets gets the same grade as an exceptionally creative project, so you don't have to worry about ranking projects that vary greatly in execution during the grading process. Students who exhibit creativity but don't meet the targets are sent the message that what truly matters is the content, not the packaging.

2. All students get a chance to explore, which positively affects their behavior. If we are going to equip our students to succeed in the 21st century, we're well-advised to give them the opportunity to explore and create (Medina, 2008; Pink, 2009; Robinson, 2001, 2009; Rshaid, 2011). As Jensen (2005) notes, curiosity and anticipation "stimulate the mental appetite" (p. 77). Exploration is central to the authentic learning experience and encourages students to use their imaginations.

When I taught a social studies class that consisted entirely of at-risk learners, I was tempted to avoid project-based learning for fear of the chaos that I thought it would invite. I could not have been more misguided; some of the most successful projects I've ever seen have come from at-risk students, who were far less likely to misbehave once engaged in completing them. When learners are not given the opportunity for adventure in the service of the curriculum, their only alternative means of excitement is disruptive behavior.

3. All learners are challenged appropriately according to their ability. Students will arrive in class with different skill sets and varying levels of ability. Just because the grading criteria are the same for all students doesn't mean that the project plans should be. When the degree of creativity employed on a project is decoupled from the grading criteria, learners are free to tackle their projects in the manner most comfortable for them. In addition, they are not locked in to the creative approach decided upon during the pre-planning state; it is always possible to consider a more or less advanced approach. If a student is doing exceptionally well on a project, you can seize on that success by gently pushing him or her to explore deeper and to imagine a more challenging outcome. Conversely, if the student is struggling at the current level, consider adjusting expectations downward in a way that still addresses the learning targets; this can both reduce stress and boost confidence.

4. A welcoming and rewarding learning environment is created. Recognizing student creativity using methods other than grades can build cohesion and community in the classroom and throughout the school. Displays, both in the class and in the hallways, are a great way to showcase student projects; so are notices in school and community newsletters. Class presentations and school assemblies are a more dramatic approach. But perhaps the single most rewarding method of recognizing the creative spirit is by communicating that recognition directly to students. Consider, for example, the feeling a student might get on receiving a note such as the following:

Ashley,

Your project was incredible! You met the learning outcomes that you set out to meet, and for that you received a very strong grade. Thank you for welcoming your classmates and me to see your passions and talents at work with clay. Your attention to detail and the depth with which you approached the topic were evident. I would be honored to display your project in the school if you feel comfortable with me doing so. I would suggest displaying it alongside your write-up so that people can understand the full context of the piece.

Thanks,
Mr. Dueck

Strategy #3: Build Measurable Creativity into the Grading Process

In some classrooms, grading standards can be designed to assess creativity very effectively. Consider the art teacher whose students range from those who need basic artistic instruction to those who are highly creative and experienced for their age. In such a case, the teacher might offer two tiers of the same course and design different learning targets for each—for example, one tier titled Foundations of Art and a more advanced tier titled Exploration of Art. The students in each tier could work in the same classroom at the same time while being challenged and graded according to different criteria. Dividing a class in this manner can reduce the temptation to lower students' grades on the basis of their relative creativity.

Of course, the reality for many educators is that dividing one course into basic and advanced tiers is simply not possible. In such a case, it's still possible to design criteria for assessing creativity. Rather than attempting to assess personal characteristics that are difficult to quantify, such as levels of ingenuity or imagination, look for results that can be identified and measured. Brookhart (2010) suggests the following such criteria for assessing students' use of creativity:

- Demonstration of a deep knowledge base
- Incorporation of new ideas
- Use of a wide variety of sources
- Use of trial and error
- Engagement in a spirit of inquiry
- Acceptance of failure as a part of learning

Brookhart provides examples of rubrics for assigning projects with the following different targeted levels of creativity: imitative, ordinary, creative, and very creative (see example in Figure 5.2). These rubrics allow students who strive for greater creativity to see the specific criteria involved.

This strategy is effective for the following reasons:

1. Projects are designed to meet each learner's needs and abilities. With this strategy, teacher expectations are dependent on the level of creativity that students choose to meet, eliminating much of the ambiguity and frustration that surrounds traditional assessments of creative work. By subdividing the class curriculum into two tiers, teachers can construct creative lessons and assignments that empower more advanced learners without frustrating their less-advanced classmates.

2. Creativity is presented as a learnable attribute that is available to everybody. Many people want to be more creative, but believe that creativity is predetermined—you either have it or you don't. Of course, this is not true. Every student has the potential to be creative (Tomlinson, 2013). By measuring the extent to which students engage in trial and error, inquiry, or research, we can help guide their creative processes. If we can assess students' abilities to add and

Figure 5.2
Analytic Rubric for Creativity

	Very Creative	Creative	Ordinary/Routine	Imitative
Depth and Quality of Ideas	Ideas represent a startling variety of important concepts from different contexts or disciplines.	Ideas represent important concepts from different contexts or disciplines.	Ideas represent important concepts from the same or similar contexts or disciplines.	Ideas do not represent important concepts.
Variety of Sources	Created product draws on a wide-ranging variety of sources, including different texts, media, resource persons, and/or personal experiences.	Created product draws on a variety of sources, including different texts, media, resource persons, and/or personal experiences.	Created product draws on a limited set of sources and media.	Created product draws on only one source, and/or sources are not trustworthy or appropriate.
Organization and Combination of Ideas	Ideas are combined in original and surprising ways to solve a problem, address an issue, or make something new.	Ideas are combined in original ways to solve a problem, address an issue, or make something new.	Ideas are combined in ways that are derived from the thinking of others (for example, of the authors in sources consulted).	Ideas are copied or restated from the source(s) consulted.
Originality of Contribution	Created product is interesting, new, and/or helpful, making an original contribution that includes identifying a previously unknown problem, issue, or purpose.	Created product is interesting, new, and/or helpful, making an original contribution for its intended purpose (e.g., solving a problem or addressing an issue).	Created product serves its intended purpose (e.g., solving a problem or addressing an issue).	Created product does not serve its intended purpose (e.g., solving a problem or addressing an issue).

Source: From *How to Create and Use Rubrics for Formative Assessment,* by S. M. Brookhart, 2013, Alexandria, VA: ASCD. Copyright 2013 by ASCD. Reprinted with permission.

subtract, we can do the same for creative pursuits. It may be tricky, but rubrics make the process much easier.

Strategy #4: Ask for Student Feedback on Tests and Use It to Inform More Creative Formatting Decisions

It is fair to say that many students do not like tests and exams, and many students with learning challenges hate the traditional assessment process entirely. When I was asked to teach a class that consisted entirely of struggling learners, this reality became clear to me immediately. Thanks to years of failure, many of my students had formed a Pavlovian reaction to tests; their behavioral issues tended to spike as tests drew nearer. To find out what caused my students the most stress on test day, I created the Test Feedback Form shown in Figure 5.3, which I would distribute to students immediately after administering the first test of the year.

When students returned the form to me, the results were clear and predictable:

- Most students had studied very little at home.
- Knowing that retesting was an option improved students' confidence.
- Students consistently indicated a preference for delivering their responses verbally or by drawing rather than through writing.

The Test Feedback Form results proved to be formative for me as a teacher. In fact, after I received the first round of results, I changed the format of the form so that it required less writing (see Figure 5.4). I also changed my testing format to include options for speaking and drawing, after which student scores improved dramatically and students appeared less stressed out on test day. If a student wished to express his or her response orally, I supplied a small voice recorder and asked him or her to record a response after the rest of the class had left the room.

Figure 5.3
World War I Test Feedback Sheet

Name: _____

1. Did you feel prepared for yesterday's test? ☐ yes ☐ no

2. Did you study outside of class time for yesterday's test? ☐ yes ☐ no

   How long? _____

3. What was your overall feeling during the test yesterday?

4. Are there parts or sections where you felt more confident than others? ☐ yes ☐ no

   Explain:

5. Did it make a difference to you knowing that you could rewrite sections where
   you did not do so well? ☐ yes ☐ no

   Explain:

6. Rank the following test formats from your most enjoyable (1) to least enjoyable (5):

   _____ multiple choice   Explain your reasons for your ranking:

   _____ written   _____

   _____ diagram/drawing   _____

   _____ spoken/oral   _____

   _____ essay/paragraph   _____

7. If you were given a chance to show your knowledge and understanding in a different way
   (a project, video, game, test of your own design, etc.), would you prefer that? ☐ yes ☐ no

   Explain:

Figure 5.4
Test Feedback Sheet

Test: _____   Name: _____

1. Did you feel **prepared** for yesterday's test?   ☐ yes   ☐ no

2. Did you study outside of class time for yesterday's test?   ☐ yes   ☐ no

   Approximately how long did you study?   _____   ☐ min   ☐ hours

3. Describe how you felt during the test yesterday:

   ☺ ☐ confident   ☐ okay   ☐ stressed
     ☐ knowledgeable   ☐ knew some stuff   ☐ my mind was blank
     ☐ calm   ☐ a little nervous ☐ rushed
     ☐ in total control   ☐ sketchy   ☐ scattered

4. Are there parts or sections where you felt more confident than others?   ☐ yes   ☐ no

   ☺ **Felt confident**   ☹ **Did NOT feel confident**
     ☐ multiple choice   ☐ multiple choice
     ☐ definitions   ☐ definitions
     ☐ short answer   ☐ short answer
     ☐ diagram   ☐ diagram
     ☐ long answer (planning section)   ☐ long answer (planning section)
     ☐ long answer (written section)   ☐ long answer (written section)

5. Did it make a difference to you knowing that you could rewrite sections
   where you did not do so well?   ☐ yes   ☐ no

   Explain:

6. Rank the following test formats from **most enjoyable (1)** to **least enjoyable (5):**

   _____ multiple choice   Explain your reasons for your ranking:

   _____ written   _____

   _____ diagram/drawing   _____

   _____ spoken/oral   _____

   _____ essay/paragraph   _____

7. If you were given a chance to show your knowledge and understanding in a different way
   (a project, video, game, test of your own design, etc.), would you prefer that?   ☐ yes   ☐ no

   PLEASE USE THE BACK OF THIS FORM IF YOU NEED TO EXPLAIN ANY RESPONSES

Here are some additional benefits of using a Test Feedback Form:

1. **Student empowerment and ownership are increased.** Many students embrace testing formats that allow them to express their responses creatively. The simple act of asking students for their opinions increases their sense of empowerment, and acting on their opinions gives teachers the opportunity to prove the importance of community in classroom decisions.

2. **The availability of a range of response modes can motivate reluctant students.** I have seen students who were unwilling to express their responses in writing confidently pick up their pencils and draw their evidence of knowledge and understanding instead.

3. **Students can demonstrate their actual knowledge.** Some learners have trouble effectively communicating their understanding using writing. Once drawing and speaking are allowed, students can access their entire range of expression. This is particularly helpful for students who struggle with English as a second language. When demonstrating understanding through drawing, students are encouraged to include key terms and descriptions to help clarify the intent of the drawing. When students respond verbally to questions, hand gestures, inflections, and facial expressions can help them to convey their meaning.

4. **The oral tradition is valued.** Allowing students to respond verbally to questions fosters

---

PERSONAL STORY

David entered the classroom each day with his skateboard in hand and a binder that looked like it had narrowly survived a battle zone. His report cards told the story of a student who had always struggled on tests. One day, when I administered a test on which students could choose either to write or draw their responses for certain questions, a curious thing happened. On the sections that allowed drawing, he scored amazingly well—and he even included written descriptions of his artwork! However, he left the final essay question blank.

It was clear to me that David had the ability to understand the essential elements of the course, but the testing formats determined his success. In the weeks that followed that first test on which he drew his responses, I built upon David's success by encouraging him to explore how he might express through writing what came so easily to him when sketching. It was not long before David was scoring full marks for both his essays and his diagrams, though he clearly still preferred to draw when given the option.

linguistic creativity and acknowledges the value of the spoken word. Storytelling precedes written language by thousands of years and may offer the respondent tools of expression and inflection unavailable through writing.

A few years back, a fellow educator challenged me about my use of oral responses on tests, arguing that oral answers could not be tracked or measured as well as written ones. In response to this challenge, I constructed the Oral Response Form shown in Figure 5.5. Using shorthand notation, this form can be filled out nearly as fast as a student can speak. The form allows you to list and rate each of the points made by students in their response. If you record students' verbal responses, you can even fill out the form after the fact.

5. Drawing responses increases engagement, confidence, and accessibility for students. Drawings help us to communicate driving directions and instructions for wiring electrical switches. Doesn't it make sense, then, that it can also help students to communicate what they've learned? I doubt that I'm the only person who skims instruction manuals for diagrams before resorting to reading the written directions.

One simple and effective way to adapt tests so that students can draw their responses is to remove the response lines following questions and have the directions read as follows: "Using sentences or a labeled drawing, describe . . . ." I encourage students to use words to enhance and clarify their drawings.

Drawings are effective instructional tools, too. My colleague Russ Reid uses political cartoons, posters, and T-shirt campaigns in his social studies lessons, then incorporates the same elements on tests— for example, by giving students the option to design a T-shirt that conveys their understanding of certain learning targets.

6. More options allow for more accurate assessment. Language arts teachers often note that if teachers of other subjects were to insist on rigorous writing standards, schools would produce more literate graduates. I could not agree more. But there is more than one way of communicating clearly. Outside of English class, the primary basis

Figure 5.5
Oral Response Form

Date: _____   Name: _____

☐ spoken only (not recorded)   ☐ recorded video   ☐ recorded audio

Location of media file: _____

Question:				
Rating of examples used in the context of the question.				**Question value:** _____
Excellent	**Good**	**Adequate**	**Not in Context/ Incorrect**	**Key Element/Detail**
Total:	Total:	Total:	Total:	Value awarded: _____
Comments:				

Russell was not the typical 12th grade history student. His grades weren't very good, and he was surprisingly candid about the difficulties he faced outside of school. However, when he was able to get to class and separate himself from some of the negative influences in his community, he showed a keen interest in history and would frequently contribute to classroom discussions.

Russell was particularly interested in warfare, so when we started a unit on World War II, I expected him to do quite well. On the day of our unit test, he shuffled into class and slumped in his chair. He seemed tired, and I noticed that his written responses on the test were very short. His dire lack of engagement was confirmed when he attempted to hand in his test halfway through class.

I quickly leafed through Russell's test after he handed it in and saw that it was mostly blank. Before he gathered up his pen and jacket and left the room, I asked him what was wrong. He told me that "it's not a writing day." Apparently his parents were involved in a nasty divorce, causing him to crash on friends' couches and depriving him of sleep.

After assuring Russell that I would get him in touch with a school counselor and that I would be able to chat with him after class about some survival strategies, I asked him if he'd be interested in using a new piece of technology I had purchased: a new iPod with a microphone attachment. I asked Russell if he'd be willing to take 30 seconds at the end of class to verbally respond to one of the test questions ("Describe reasons why Britain was successful against Germany in the Battle of Britain."). He agreed, so I asked him to stick around until class was over and take a nap in the meantime. He placed his head on the desk and promptly fell asleep. *(cont.)*

for grading is evidence of learning, not language ability, spelling, grammar, or sentence structure. The ultimate goal is always to assess student knowledge and understanding.

Strategy #5: Use the "I Know I Am Close" Multiple-Choice Response Format to Promote Creative Thinking

"Growth comes from being surrounded by critical friends." Never was this aphorism proven more accurate than the time I formed a discussion team in our school district focused on the topics of assessment for learning and sound grading challenges. One of the people I had dragged onto the team of 10 educators was Ben Arcuri, a senior chemistry teacher from a neighboring high school. I had taught with Ben in two other schools, and I knew him to be critical of his practice, unafraid to ask tough questions, and more candid than most when expressing frustration.

Near the end of one of our meetings, Ben raised a concern. I have tried my best to capture the essence of the account:

I'm all fine and dandy with the *concept* behind assessment for learning—how we should have students know the prescribed learning outcomes and make projects that they can self- and peer-assess. But for me, there's a lot more to it than airy-fairy projects. My chemistry course has a major exam with a lot of multiple-choice questions. Multiple choice is probably the most common testing format around because it's so easy to administer and grade.

For this reason, I predict that it'll increasingly be mandated by governments for use in schools. If we want to actually achieve assessment for learning, what are we going to do with multiple choice? Each student picks an answer, and either it's right or it's wrong—there's no value in being close. In fact, a student could narrow it down to the two most likely answers, knowing all there is to know about the question, but choose the lesser of the two best options and still get zero points! Multiple choice is a case of all or nothing. If we're for learning, what are we going to do about that?

We all left the meeting with Ben's challenge still hanging in the air, and I soon came face to face with a vivid illustration of the all-or-nothing multiple-choice conundrum. On my way home, my wife called me and asked that I pick something up for her. Unable to write as I was driving, I told her I would try my best to remember the directions. I listened intently to her and took careful mental notes. I ended up finding the right street, but couldn't remember the exact address. I was thinking of calling my wife back when I remembered Ben's dilemma. I imagined that my attempt to find the right address was a multiple-choice test, with giant letters hanging from the sky above four buildings in town: one on the distant horizon, another far across town, and another two clustered closely together on the street I was on. I then imagined that I only had one chance to choose the correct house. If forced to choose between the massive letters *A* and *C* that drifted in the breeze above my head, I was stuck.

Though I was in the right part of town and even on the right street, I still had only a 50/50 chance of getting the answer either completely right or completely wrong. If I chose the incorrect buildings on the correct street, I would score no better than if I had driven off over the horizon. How frustrating!

In the end, after much collaboration and discussion, our team came up with a solution to Ben's challenge in the form of the I Know I Am Close response format for multiple-choice questions. This format allows students to offer two answers instead of just one, as long as they also provide an explanation for choosing them both. Such a format lets students show their understanding in a much more fine-grained way than does the traditional single-answer format, especially in cases when students

- Know for certain that some of the responses are not correct, but are unclear as to the best answer.
- Are confused by ambiguous or otherwise challenging wording.
- Can recall an unresolved classroom debate about the issue.
- Have a well-thought-out opinion that differs from the conventional wisdom.

Our team designed a multiple-choice response sheet that includes room for up to two answers for each question, plus space for an explanation (see Figure 5.6). For automated or online testing, a supplemental sheet could be provided (see Figure 5.7).

I have tended to institute a limit of five dual-response answers per test. There's usually not enough time for students to offer two responses plus an explanation for every question, and giving them the option can lead them to overthink unnecessarily. You may also consider asking students to indicate the one response that they believe is most likely correct—such as by circling the letter or number—even in cases when two responses are offered.

With this type of format, what is paramount is the evidence of understanding provided, not simply the letter selected. Explanations will either receive a point, a half-point, or no point at all depending on

Figure 5.6
Multiple-Choice Response Sheet

Name: _____

Write the letter that corresponds to the correct answer in the first space provided below. If you are unsure of your answer, write the letter that represents your second choice in the second blank. SUGGESTION: Select no more than five "second choices" or you may run out of time.

1. ____ ____	11. ____ ____	21. ____ ____
2. ____ ____	12. ____ ____	22. ____ ____
3. ____ ____	13. ____ ____	23. ____ ____
4. ____ ____	14. ____ ____	24. ____ ____
5. ____ ____	15. ____ ____	25. ____ ____
6. ____ ____	16. ____ ____	26. ____ ____
7. ____ ____	17. ____ ____	27. ____ ____
8. ____ ____	18. ____ ____	28. ____ ____
9. ____ ____	19. ____ ____	
10. ____ ____	20. ____ ____	**TOTAL:** _____

On the lines below, provide some information that explains why you are unsure of the correct response.

____. _____

____. _____

____. _____

____. _____

____. _____

____. _____

Figure 5.7
Supplemental Multiple-Choice Response Form

Please include this sheet with your multiple-choice response form. If the original multiple-choice responses were completed digitally or online, check this box: ☐

Name: _____ Date: _____ Test: _____

For each question below, indicate the two responses you are considering by shading in the corresponding boxes. You must use the **explanation area** to describe why you are struggling to determine the correct response. Share why you might consider both responses to be correct. Make an effort to demonstrate your understanding of the concept. You may use a combination of words and diagrams.

Question: _____ Responses to consider: ☐ A ☐ B ☐ C ☐ D

Explanation Area:

If I had to select ONE response only, I would choose _____.

Question: _____ Responses to consider: ☐ A ☐ B ☐ C ☐ D

Explanation Area:

If I had to select ONE response only, I would choose _____.

the extent to which they demonstrate real understanding. It is a good idea to stress this fact to students before administering the test.

Here are a few reasons for using the I Know I Am Close multiple-choice response format:

1. Teachers gain insight into their students' answer-selection process. A good set of multiple-choice questions should induce serious contemplation in students. If we are indeed assessing *for learning,* knowing what considerations students are grappling with in stressful test situations is very valuable.

2. Multiple-choice tests become more than just guessing games. The I Know I Am Close format encourages students to use the higher-order thinking skill of metacognition—that is, thinking about their own thinking. Students who are trying to decide on a correct answer have the opportunity to explore the reasons for their indecision in writing, so that their metacognition is documented. Consider one student's opinion of this system:

> I like it! I mean, at first I used it, and then as I went through the test, I thought back to the two selections. Using prior knowledge, I was going through the test, and *ahh*—EPIPHANY! I went back and selected only one answer. So I used it, but really only to think more about it, and then in the end I did not use it at all.

3. The format addresses potential language barriers. A study by Cassels and Johnstone (1984) found that more challengingly worded questions accounted for a 10 percent increase in errors on multiple-choice tests. As Burton, Sudweeks, Merrill, and Wood (1991) note,

> If the vocabulary is somewhat difficult, the item will likely measure reading ability in addition to the achievement of the objective for which the item was written. As a result, poor readers who have achieved the objective may receive scores indicating that they have not. Use difficult and technical vocabulary only when essential for measuring the objective. (p. 31)

A number of years ago, the final essay question on British Columbia's 11th grade social studies exam asked students to write about Canada's emerging autonomy in the 20th century. The people grading essays that year were surprised to find that many students had instead written about the history of the *automobile* in Canada. Similar comprehension issues might go unnoticed by teachers without clues in the form of student explanations to help identify the confusion. Those less familiar with the language and its structures might benefit immensely from a linguistic safety net—or at least from the opportunity to explain what they know!

4. The format can guide revision. Consider the following question from a math test:

Solve the following problem: $6 + 3 \times 4 - 2$
A. 0
B. 16
C. 18
D. 34

In this case, each of the listed responses is the inevitable result of a different solution strategy, only one of which is correct. According to the order of operations, the correct response is *B,* 16, but incorrect answers offer clues as to the students' thinking. (For example, students who select *C,* 18, are probably adding 3 to 6 and subtracting 2 from 4 before multiplying the results of the two equations.) The I Know I Am Close format allows students to self-identify the questions that are causing them the most difficulty (see Figure 5.8 for an example).

5. The format helps identify problematic questions. Shortly after our educator team designed the I Know I Am Close format, I used it on a unit test about the Paris Peace Conference in my 12th grade history class. The test included a question that I'd used on this particular test over many years:

Figure 5.8
Sample Student Explanation to Math Question Using the I Know I Am Close Format

Solve the following problem: $6 + 3 \times 4 - 2$
A. 0
B. 16
C. 18
D. 34

Responses to consider: ☐ A ■ B ☐ C ■ D

Explanation Area:

I think that the correct answer is 16 because I multiply the 3 and 4 and I get 12. Then I add the 6 and I get 18. Then the question is 18 – 2 and that equals 16.

What I find confusing is that I was studying with Marie yesterday and she said that we just read it like a book from left to right. If I did that, I would do this:

6 + 3 = 9 then 9 × 4 = 36 then 36 – 2 = 34

But I think the answer really is 16.

If I had to select ONE response only, I would choose letter <u>B</u>.

After 1919, which country controlled the Saar coal region?

A. The United States

B. Japan

C. Germany

D. France

I had always assumed that the correct answer to this question was *D,* France; as I discussed with my students in class, Germany was forced to concede the coal from the Saar region for a period of five years following 1919. When I collected the unit test on which I inaugurated the I Know I Am Close format, I was shocked to see that more students had chosen to debate this question than any other. Here are some of the student responses to the questions:

Answer: C. Germany. The question only states "After 1919," not how long after. France only had limited control for a period of five years following the 1919 Conference. Since 1919, with the exception of those five years, the control over this area has belonged to Germany.

Answer: C. Germany. Germany was allowed to keep the land, and only lost the coal. The word "control" is debatable and requires context.

Answer: A. The United States. Woodrow Wilson championed the notion of self-determination. On the basis of this concept, the French were unsuccessful in their bid to take full control of the Saar region, and therefore it remained under the German flag. Considering the influence that Wilson had over this decision, it could be argued that the United States inevitably controlled the region in the years following 1919.

I soon noticed that the most capable students in class were the ones most eager to offer Germany and the United States as alternative responses, suggesting that the question wasn't written as clearly as I—the test designer—had thought. A little rewording and the intent would have been much clearer. The following year, I changed the question to read as follows: "In the five years following 1919, which country controlled the coal of the Saar region?" The clear answer to this version of the question is *D,* France.

Nearly every teacher I know who has used the I Know I Am Close format has also found that when multiple students have trouble selecting among responses, it is often because the question is poorly worded. In these cases, it's evident that students are not lacking in content knowledge, but rather struggling with ambiguous language.

6. All learners benefit. As noted above, the I Know I Am Close format can be engaging for the most capable students in class. However, it is also beneficial for students who struggle with reading, who need only eliminate two of the four options as long as they explain their thinking. One at-risk student who took the previously cited test on the Paris Peace Conference explained that he would have been able to determine the correct response to a question if he'd only known the meaning of the word *obligated.*

7. Test anxiety and stress are reduced. The wrong types of stress can inhibit our ability to recall information (Schmidt & Schwabe, 2011). The amount of control the students have over their responses to test questions can vary tremendously, from a lot of control on essay questions to relatively little on multiple-choice questions. The I Know I Am Close format helps students to establish greater control over the latter. As one of my students, Rheanna, put it, the format "made [the test experience] a lot less stressful. I get pretty worked up about tests, especially when I know I am really close to the right answer. This option made it a lot better." Another student, Kendall, noted, "When I know I am close, it is nice to know it is not all or nothing. Sometimes two responses can appear to be correct, depending on how one might read the question. I love having the chance to explain."

One of our duties as test designers is to make tests as user-friendly and accessible as we can. I have not seen any standards or prescribed learning outcomes requiring teachers to be tricky, vague, or misleading. Considering the amount of stress that students experience on test day, we, as educators, might be wise to look for ways to increase confidence rather than erode it.

Using Modern Technology to Encourage Creativity

Anyone who hasn't been living under a rock for the last few years knows how much emerging technologies are changing the landscape of education. Each of the following classroom strategies using popular applications can help teachers to foster creativity among students in the digital age.

Strategy #1: Use Twitter for Class Discussions and Tests

The idea is simple: the teacher poses a question or problem to the class, and the students must tweet back their responses. Because tweets are limited to 140 characters or fewer, students are challenged to state their cases and mount any rebuttals as concisely as possible. The Twitter feed can be tracked by using a hashtag unique to the class (e.g., #MrDueckHistory) and projected onto a large screen at the front of the class. Another option is to institute Twitter Tuesdays, during the last 10 minutes of which students are to converse entirely via Twitter. (If devices allowing access to Twitter are scarce, students can respond in groups.)

On some of his tests, my colleague Russ Reid gives students the option to submit their answers in Twitter format. Figure 5.9 shows an

Figure 5.9
Sample Question Using Twitter Format

1. Create a Twitter conversation (four tweets) between two of the earth's spheres. (4 points)
2. The spheres are to discuss the effect of deforestation on their sphere.
3. Each sphere needs a handle, and you must include one hashtag that relates to the conversation.

@troposphere123: how's the oxygen & CO2 today? #atrisk

@biosphere: fine, but running out of forest #atrisk #gettingwarmer

@troposphere123: 2 much deforestation #atrisk #gettingwarmer #actsoon

@biosphere: need to selectively log, reforest, cut back on cars #atrisk #gettingwarmer #timerunningout

example of one such question, in which students were asked to supply a Twitter dialogue between two of the earth's spheres, including relevant user names and hashtags.

Here are some reasons for using this strategy in the classroom:

1. The medium is trendy and appealing to students. Students are using shorthand and symbols to communicate in everyday life, so using the Twitter format in class acknowledges its validity as a form of expression.

2. The medium enforces efficiency. Tweets must be no more than 140 characters in length, so students are forced to get to the point. When students must focus on the essential elements to convey understanding, teachers end up having to wade through less material when grading.

3. The medium is equitable and always in flux. As my colleague Scott Harkness taught me, Twitter-based class discussion allows all learners to engage in the conversation. The loudest voices in the class must conform to the same standards as those who are more reserved. There is room for divergent points of view, and the conversation moves at a quick pace. New ideas and arguments continually replace the existing ones, and relevant points made earlier can be quickly retweeted if necessary.

Strategy #2: Use Digital Photos and Videos to Enhance Class Discussions

Ask students to collect photos or other examples related to a concept discussed in class. For example, my colleague Russ Reid asked his geography students to find examples of geographic features discussed in class; another colleague, Shona Becker, asked her students to collect photos of fractions around the school grounds and present them to the class for discussion. Chemistry teacher Ben Arcuri asked his students to collect photos or video footage of terms related to chemistry; he awarded points according to the difficulty of capture, so that evidence of *data, observations,* and *experiments* received only 1 or 2 points, but evidence of *hypotheses, theories,* and *vapor pressure* garnered 15 points apiece. In some cases the students found actual examples, and in other cases they filmed themselves acting out chemical reactions. In every instance, students were learning from each other. (The activity sheet for Mr. Arcuri's assignment is shown in Figure 5.10.)

Here are some reasons for using photos and videos in classroom assignments:

1. The process is engaging for students. Students love to take photos. The prospect of creating instantaneous images using our phones is alluring, just as Polaroid cameras used to be. It is easy to engage students in an activity that has them collect images of themselves and each other.

2. Students love to share their creations. In this strategy, students get to show off their photo and video collections in front of classmates. Mixing in content knowledge with socializing can make for a highly engaging activity.

3. Students learn and review content in the context of their own community. Students increase their consciousness of place when they are tasked with finding examples of content in their very own environment.

Strategy #3: Use Applications to Perform In-Depth Analysis of Digital Content

A number of apps on the market allow students and teachers not only to capture photos and videos, but also to analyze them using tools previously reserved for analysts on television. Students can now be little John Maddens, employing slow motion, arrows, lines, and commentary to analyze their or their classmates' work. Teachers can record students' class presentations and append comments and suggestions to the recordings later; they can then e-mail, text, or upload their analyses to students for immediate viewing. Both Coach's Eye (www.coachseye.com) and

Figure 5.10
Sample Assignment Incorporating Digital Photos

In groups of two or three, use an iPad or phone to take pictures and label examples of each of the following terms. The same picture can be used for multiple terms.

The terms are worth different points. The group with the most points at the end of class will win a yummy glass of iced tea.

If you have the same picture of a term as another group, both teams will fail to get points for that term. So . . . NO SHARING.

The terms will be discussed and the text questions will be completed during the next class.

Sec 3.1

Read pages 41 to 48 for the definitions.

Define:

Qualitative	(2 points)	Quantitative	(2 points)
Observation	(1 point)	Interpretation	(5 points)
Description	(1 point)	Data	(1 point)
Experiment	(2 points)	Hypothesis	(15 points)
Theory	(15 points)	Law	(5 points)

Complete questions #1–6 on page 43.

Sec 3.2

Define:

Matter	(1 point)	Substance	(1 point)
Physical Property	(5 points)	Chemical Property	(10 points)
Intensive Property	(10 points)	Extensive Property	(5 points)

Complete questions #13 and 15 on page 45.

What are the three common states of matter? List the set of properties of each.

Name four exotic states of matter (2 million points each).

Define:

Hardness	(2 points)	Malleability	(2 points)
Ductile	(2 points)	Luster	(2 points)
Viscosity	(2 points)	Diffusion	(2 points)
Vapor	(10 points)	Vapor Pressure	(10 points)

Complete questions #21, 22, 24, and 25 on page 48.

Source: Courtesy Ben Arcuri. Reprinted with permission.

Ubersense (www.ubersense.com) allow users to capture good examples against which students can compare their own work (e.g., speeches by Martin Luther King Jr. for a unit on public speaking). Imagine, rather than hauling home 30 large multimedia projects to grade, scrolling through them all on your sofa while holding nothing but an iPad in your hands. Now that's what I call grading smarter, not harder!

Here are some more reasons for employing digital analysis techniques in the classroom:

1. It works! The halftime football analysts know it, and so do the nightly newscasters: whenever footage is slowed down and combined with commentary, the audience is afforded a chance to view things from a new angle.

2. Analysis is easily shared. Apps designed to analyze photo or video usually enable files to be shared with ease; users can often distribute or upload material with a simple click.

3. Technology is personalized. The introduction of VCRs and DVD players allowed students to view documentaries and movie clips on demand. Personal computers and the Internet allowed access to information as never before. Now, students are able to manipulate and personalize material in ways that would have been unimaginable just a short time ago.

Strategy #4: Use Online Document Management Systems

Google Docs (https://docs.google.com) is one example of an online document management system that allows users to collect and display large amounts of formative assessment data in a short period of time. This type of system lets you quickly produce forms consisting of any combination of standard question types, including true/false, multiple-choice, checklist, and open-ended. Students can access the documents via hyperlink using phones, tablets, or computers, and teachers can view the subsequent grading data in table form or in more graphic formats like pie charts.

The Edmodo system (www.edmodo.com) is more specifically geared to education. It allows teachers to design online quizzes in multiple-choice or fill-in-the-blank formats and automatically grades students' results as soon as they are finished.

Here are some reasons for including online document management systems in your classroom:

1. Immediate feedback guides instruction. Feedback using these systems is prompt and accurate, allowing teachers to adapt follow-up activities accordingly. If it is obvious from a glance at a data-results pie chart that most students are on the right track, teachers can feel free to move on to covering other elements of the content.

2. Systems facilitate formative assessment. Online assessments using document management systems can clearly measure how well students know the selected material.

3. Handheld devices allow for instantaneous responses. Many handheld wireless products, known commonly as responders, are available for students to use for individually responding to questions. And with an increasing number of students owning smartphones, schools will soon reap the budgetary benefits of the BYOD (Bring Your Own Device) era.

Conclusion

Most people would agree that exploration, creativity, and invention are effective avenues to authentic learning experiences. Yet teachers very often don't feel comfortable venturing into the realm of creativity unless they feel that they can accurately assess the degree of creativity on display. If engagement is the key to unlocking the learning potential of students, then projects that allow students to blend their personal interests with prescribed learning outcomes should be encouraged. In my own case, I quickly realized that I only needed to measure the learning outcomes of assignments, regardless of the creativity involved—yet as I broadened the window through which students could demonstrate understanding, the learning environment improved dramatically for everyone.

Frequently Asked Questions

Q: With all the content that I need to cover, how do I find the time for my students to complete projects and unique assignments?

A: I once heard a conference presenter use a clever analogy to address this issue. If you arrive home from a hardware store with a wonderful new tool and find that there is no more room in your toolbox, you may need to throw away something old to make room for the new. To find the time for increased creativity, I look for ways to deliver content in less time-consuming ways. For example, I have reduced the number of notes students are required to take from the board; I now ask students to read up on the big ideas, and then I use video, hands-on activities, and classroom conversations to fill in the details.

Q: State or provincial requirements force me to maintain a rigid test structure. How can I introduce creative assignments when I need to report on prescribed learning outcomes?

A: For far too long, we have assumed that traditional testing is more accurate than other forms of assessments. Creative projects can be incredibly effective for assessing the extent to which students understand learning objectives. What matters is that assessments are authentic, personal, and focused on the learning objectives. Get students involved in identifying the objectives before starting on a project and regularly revisit the objectives to ensure that students are on track to addressing them.

Q: If universities require students to meet stringent testing standards, why waste time on creative assessments?

A: There are many myths about what universities most value and uphold in education. Alberti (2012) points to surveys suggesting that postsecondary instructors value a deeper sense of understanding over a broad, survey-style approach to covering content. (As Albert Einstein put it, "Any fool can know; the point is to understand.") My former grade 12 English teacher turned writer and editor, Dianne Hildebrand, has spent her lifetime gauging the pulse of education and the facilitation of learning. Consider the following quote from a conversation she had with university professor and author Florentine Strzelczyk:

> Even a less-than-in-depth look at university curricula and preferred methodology reveals that creativity plays a crucial role. In academia today, exploration, originality, creativity and discovery are particularly valued. You will not distinguish yourself in academia these days by merely knowing a whole lot of information—which is free on the Internet. You distinguish yourself by being able to apply this knowledge to new contexts creatively and by uncovering knowledge gaps.

Q: If I have large classes, can I have students complete creative assignments in groups?

A: There is great value in having students collaborate and share in a learning experience. Group projects instill and enforce many qualities that are critical to success in future endeavors, including communication, group organization, consensus, and compromise. However, group activities too often fail to give an accurate picture of each individual student's ability (O'Connor, 2010). Slapping a group grade on a collection of individual contributions is probably not an accurate form of assessment. Ideally, teachers should identify the individual contributions of students to a given group effort. Of course, not everything requires a grade; some projects can be completed simply for fun and adventure.

Q: My projects do not meet core standards like my tests do. How can I switch to project-based learning and report accurately?

A: You may have to redesign your projects to align with the core standards. Commit to assessing only the learning objectives, regardless of the media in which they are presented. You can even have students contribute to the design of the rubric that you will use to assess the projects.

CONCLUSION

When I first started making grading and assessment changes in my classroom, I had no idea that the most profound side effects would center on relationships. I thought building a simple unit plan would be a good way to let my students know what they were about to learn. What I didn't know was that I was about to introduce a host of changes to the way I interacted with my students and that my role in the classroom was also going to change. I didn't know that student-monitored retesting would dramatically alter the educational trajectories of many of my students, or that eliminating zeros for missed assignments would also remove a key barrier to student success (especially for those living with poverty), or that getting rid of late penalties would greatly alleviate student stress. I undertook these changes for reasons related to *teaching,* never realizing the effect they would have on my *relationships* with students.

Student Challenges

Many students have home lives that make it difficult for them to succeed in school and almost impossible for them to nurture positive relationships. As a high school administrator, I regularly have a front-row seat to family crises. It is increasingly likely that the only active parent of a child living in poverty is a single mother with a low level of education (McLanahan, 2004; Schwartz & Mare, 2005).

A girl was recently referred to my office for refusing to participate in P.E. class. During our conversation, she shared with me the following details of her living situation:

> Every time my mom gets a new boyfriend, we move. She pays for his habits and I get to sleep in a closet. I don't get a lot of sleep. . . . I really wish we hadn't been evicted from our last place. . . . After I fight with my mom and her boyfriend, I don't want to go to school—I just don't care.

Students from low-income and drug-affected households face a range of challenges that go well beyond cramped living spaces. Drug and alcohol abuse lead to violence and food shortages. Our local police and intervention workers know certain students all too well because they live in homes that repeatedly erupt in domestic disputes. In many homes, scarce finances are diverted to meth, cocaine, and vodka rather than basic food needs; as Jensen (2013) notes, lack of basic nutritional sustenance is one of the most pronounced barriers to behavioral and academic success.

Of course, family issues and community pressures are not reserved for students from low-income families. Teaching a senior-leadership class at my high school has enlightened me to the challenges faced by some of our most successful students. Many of these students face immense pressure to succeed, which can have negative repercussions of its own.

The Importance of Relationships in the School Community

Young people benefit academically from positive relationships with adults and peers (Pletka, 2007). Strong social supports also play a pivotal role in helping people recover from stressful situations (King, King, Fairbank, Keane, & Adams, 1998) and maintaining strong physical and psychological health (Southwick & Charney, 2013). Relationships are critical to the growth and development of the human brain (Gunnar & Cheatham, 2003; Lupien et al., 2011; Seigal, 2012). Unfortunately, many students do not have a variety of consistent, positive avenues through which to form attachments with well-intentioned adults. Membership in the Boy Scouts is roughly half of what it was in 1972 (Banks, 2010), church attendance is down (Olson, 2009), and many community-based sports clubs have become too expensive for low-income families (Datko, 2011). The vexing question emerges: if not at school, where can we expect young people to form positive relationships with adults and with each other? By implementing grading and assessment changes at school, we can profoundly affect the quality of relationships among all members of the school community.

Teacher-Student Relationships

Students are quick to determine whether or not an environment is built upon an equitable foundation. When an environment feels hostile to them or when there is an obvious power imbalance, many young people seek to reduce their discomfort by engaging in disruptive behavior. Such acting out can be compounded when students face grading consequences due to issues outside of their control. Consider, for example, a student who receives a zero on an assignment that his alcoholic father tore up in a drunken rage. The injustice of the grade will only serve to fuel the student's anger and frustration. At a time when the student most needs positive relationships with adults in his life, the student is subjected to impersonal academic penalties designed to teach a lesson or to encourage compliance.

Because it is impossible for us to know the living conditions of all our students, we need to adopt grading routines that support all students, regardless of their home environments. When grading policies are designed to be accurate, fair, and considerate, they can support positive relationships between teachers and students. The following three actions are particularly crucial for strengthening such relationships:

1. Eliminating grading rules that penalize students for behavioral infractions and predicaments outside of their control.
2. Designing assessments that improve student confidence by promoting improved understanding of learning outcomes.
3. Increasing student ownership and voice in the area of assessment.

Sound grading practices can provide a safety net for students who are living with challenges that are unknown to the adults in the school. When we eliminate unfair grading policies, students get the message that we value their achievement. Confidence and self-esteem are strengthened when students' scores improve. Providing students a channel through which they can assess themselves and their peers encourages reflective learning.

Uniform homework inevitably leads to conflict between teachers and students. Consider a student who fought with his mom over a homework assignment late into the evening and never ended up completing it. When this student returns to school the following morning, he can expect to receive a zero on the assignment. Concerned about his social status, the student probably won't let anyone know that he and his mom tried and failed to complete the homework; instead, he's much more likely to declare the assignment itself to be stupid. If he is removed from class, he will have at least enjoyed insulting the teacher who trod upon his dignity and maybe earned some social currency in the process. Remember, when students have to choose between social status and academic concerns, they almost always choose the former (Geary, 2011).

Some students view conventional testing and assessment routines as contradictory to school values. One of my students, Bryan, had ample opportunity to take advantage of the retesting system I instituted in class. Over the years, I came to admire his exceptional reflectiveness. During the last week of Bryan's senior year, I asked him what he thought of the retesting system. Here's how he responded:

> Testing is a cold, calculated experience. In my opinion, it's in contrast to what school is supposed to be all about. Every day seems to be a happy day until we arrive at test day, and suddenly a different teacher seems to enter the room. Everything turns cutthroat, all about the rules—you have one chance to get things right. The teacher may as well say, "That guy over there figured it out before you did, he got it right on the day he was supposed to, so we're ranking him higher." I'm not suggesting that students should take retest after retest—that is impractical. But at least give them one more chance to show what they know and don't know. The idea is to learn, not be punished for not learning faster. I think the way to describe your retesting system would be as "friendship with authority."

Student-Parent Relationships

The vast majority of parents want the best for their children. Unfortunately, both applying and receiving pressure to perform can often lead to chronic stress and, eventually, resignation among parents and students. Too many times I've called up a parent to discuss a student only to hear, "Do whatever you want. I am done with that kid."

When students feel that they are unable to learn, they often resort to truancy and disruptive behavior (Wiliam & Black, 1998). Such actions can lead to an increase in confrontations between students and adults both in school and at home. However, when these students suddenly encounter academic success, student-parent relationships improve. Consider the following statements from the parent of one student, Jon, describing his behavior before we instituted changes to our assessment process:

> My expectations of Jon coming into high school were slim to none. Things were just going to be bigger and worse. It was to the point where he just didn't care what the consequences were. I thought, "Here we go, we're toast. We're never going to get through this." He was in trouble at home, so the grounding starts, the pulling of the Xbox and Nintendo and all the good stuff he likes. So then he's mad, I'm mad—it was just day in and day out.
>
> For the longest time, if Jon thought he was going to fail at something, he wouldn't try it. He would rather not try it and face the consequences than try it and fail at it.

When we introduced retesting and eliminated behavioral grades, Jon experienced greater academic success, which in turn led to a sharp decline in behavioral infractions. These positive results greatly improved Jon's relationship with his mother at home. Here are her recollections of his transformation:

> He got more confidence and he thought he would at least try assignments and tests and worry about the consequences after. Now he's on the honor roll! He takes physics and chemistry and all those things that I never dreamed he would take.
>
> I'm not worried anymore. He's come so far. Like I've been telling him for two years, when he walks across that stage with that hat and gown on, I will be in the front row bawling like a 5-year-old. I can see it; it is going to happen.

Student-Student Relationships

During much of my career, I would assign a single overall score to group projects, regardless of who did what. I'm a little baffled as to why it took me so long to change this routine, given that I sensed from the beginning that group scores were neither accurate nor equitable. When students are instead assessed on their individual contributions to collaborative assignments, there is less room for conflict among them about who deserves more or less credit.

Assessment methods that foster increased student ownership and engagement can provide a stage upon which students can shine in front of their peers. As one of my at-risk students put it, "Students just want to show off in front of each other."

Punitive grading unfortunately casts a spotlight on socioeconomic inequality among students. Frustration can boil over if students feel that assessment policies penalize them for situations that are beyond their control, leading to a potentially hostile environment. When returning tests to my at-risk class, I noticed that interpersonal student conflict was more pronounced when students anticipated that they were going to receive low test results.

Many students have very negative opinions of their own academic abilities—a sentiment that, unfortunately, is often reinforced by peers. When I was assigned to teach an 11th grade class that consisted entirely of at-risk students, I was shocked by the way students spoke about their own abilities. The first student to enter the room sat as far away from me as he could and mumbled an inaudible response to my greetings; when the second student entered the room, the first student exclaimed, "Hey stupid, sit over here! We can both suck at this course." When the third student entered the room, the second student said, "Nice, all three of us are in here! I won't be the dumbest now that he just walked in." When the fourth student arrived and saw his classmates, he took on a look of resignation and remarked, "Oh, this must be the failure class." I knew in that instant that I would have to change

PERSONAL STORY

When I first began offering students retests, I did so by interviewing students about whatever topic they wished to retest. One of the first students to take me up on this offer was Melinda. When she arrived for our interview, she waited patiently in the hallway as I finished up another meeting. When we finally sat down together, Melinda fidgeted a little but appeared otherwise confident. I asked her a series of questions about the topic she wished to retest—the role of women in the 1920s. In her answers, Melinda demonstrated an excellent grasp of 1920s terminology and a solid understanding of the gains that women experienced at that time.

When she was done, Melinda asked me how I thought she had performed. I responded that she had answered the questions flawlessly and that I would be revising her mark on the test's long-answer question to reflect a perfect score. As she was leaving the room, she paused by the door and addressed me.

"This is probably the only class I'm putting effort into," she said.

"Why is that?" I asked.

"Because I get to see what I'm right about and what I'm not right about. This helps me get my grades up. It makes me feel smarter than I really am—I mean, I don't get good grades, but in this class I know things and I feel smart. I haven't really felt smart in the past."

As Melinda left the room and the sound of her footsteps faded into the weekend, I couldn't think of a better way to end a Friday afternoon.

my routines if I was to alter the damning script that so easily rolled off the tongues of these unfortunate learners.

At other times, I saw struggling students encourage each other and promote academic achievement through the retesting system. One day, as I watched two students walk out of the classroom, I saw one of them smack the other on the back and say, "You better go in for that retest, man! You could nail that section." The boy took his friend's advice; after making many positive choices, he went on to win the award for top history student in the school. You could hear a hundred necks crack at our year-end awards ceremony when I read his name aloud as a major winner. I could imagine people thinking, "Students like that simply don't get these awards! This must be a mistake." But this student had the skills and the ability; what he most needed was a system that recognized his abilities and would bend on the days when life required it.

Student Self-Concepts

The most important relationship is the one that a student has with him- or herself as a learner. When students believe that they are capable of learning successfully, they are better able to actually do so, whereas those who are resigned to failure will be likely to have their pessimism confirmed. However, these self-concepts can change: I have seen students enter my class resigned to failure and marveled as they evolved into confident, empowered learners.

These transformations have undoubtedly been the most rewarding experiences of my grading and assessment journey.

Embracing Change

Change is not easy. Sometimes it can make us feel quite isolated. My hope is that some of you reading this book will feel empowered to take on challenges that previously seemed too daunting. By blending sound grading and assessment for learning practices, we can better identify and measure learning outcomes.

My grading and assessment journey is ongoing. The urging of my administrator, Tom Schimmer, and the work of Rick Stiggins and Ken O'Connor influenced me to get the journey started. As it progressed, my school administration provided me with support when I needed it, and colleagues offered me invaluable formative feedback. Most importantly, learners from across the spectrum have told me what works for them and what does not. These students have provided me with a window into their lives and shown me what assessment changes have increased their confidence the most. Thankfully, these students are now challenging the very notion of traditional school success.

It is exciting to realize that some of the assumptions underlying our mind-sets as established educators aren't necessarily true. A 21st-century approach to education must be less about rigor and more about deeper learning, less about enticing students with the currency of grades and much more about building engaged and vibrant learning communities. It is about preparing students for their real futures rather than the artificial ones that we have long claimed to understand, about designing effective consequences and behavioral interventions rather than simply leaning on penalties that students end up ignoring. As educators, our most enduring legacy is in the relationships that we form with the students in our care—and in this area, our approach to assessment can make all the difference.

REFERENCES

Alberti, S. (2012). Making the shifts. *Educational Leadership, 70*(4), 24–27.

Anderson, A. (2011). Towering targets: Why the ball looks bigger when you're on your game. *Scientific American Mind, 22*(3), 6.

Banks, D. (2010). After 100 years, are the Boy Scouts still relevant? Available: http://archive.wired.com/geekdad/2010/02/boy-scouts-at-100-years/

Beghetto, R. A., & Kaufman, J. C. (2013). Fundamentals of creativity. *Educational Leadership, 70*(5), 10–15.

Blachnio, A., & Weremko, M. (2011). Academic cheating is contagious: The influence of the presence of others on honesty. *International Journal of Applied Psychology, 1*(1), 14–19.

Black, P., & Wiliam, D. (1998). Assessment and classroom learning. *Assessment in Education, 5*(1), 70–74.

Bradshaw, J. (2012). Why university students need a well-rounded education. *The Globe and Mail.* Available: http://www.theglobeandmail.com/news/national/time-to-lead/why-university-students-need-a-well-rounded-education/article4610406/?page=all

Brodie, R. (2004). *Virus of the mind: The new science of the meme.* New York: Hay House.

Brookhart, S. M. (2010). *How to assess higher-order thinking skills in your classroom.* Alexandria, VA: ASCD.

Brookhart, S. M. (2013). *How to create and use rubrics for formative assessment and grading.* Alexandria, VA: ASCD.

Brooks, J. G., & Dietz, M. E. (2012). The dangers and opportunities of the common core. *Educational Leadership, 70*(4), 64–67.

Brownlie, F., & King, J. (2011). *Learning in safe schools: Creating classrooms where all students belong* (2nd ed.). Markham, Ontario: Pembroke.

Bryant, A. (2013). Corner office: In head-hunting, big data may not be such a big deal. *The New York Times.* Available: http://www.nytimes.com/2013/06/20/business/in-head-hunting-big-data-may-not-be-such-a-big-deal.html?pagewanted=all&_r=0

Burton, S. J., Sudweeks, R. R., Merrill, P. F., & Wood, B. (1991). *How to prepare multiple-choice test items: Guidelines for university faculty.* Provo, UT: Brigham Young University Testing Services and the Department of Instructional Science.

Cassels, J. R. T., & Johnstone, A. H. (1984). The effect of language on student performance on multiple-choice tests in chemistry. *Journal of Chemical Education, 61*(7), 613–615.

Chappuis, J., Stiggins, R., Chappuis, S., & Arter, J. (2012). *Classroom assessment for student learning: Doing it right, using it well* (2nd ed.). New York: Pearson.

Cho, H., Hallfors, D. D., & Sanchez, V. (2005). Evaluation of a high school peer group intervention for at-risk youth. *Journal of Abnormal Child Psychology, 33*(3), 363–374.

Cooper, D. (2011). *Redefining fair: How to plan, assess, and grade for excellence in mixed-ability classrooms.* Bloomington, IN: Solution Tree.

Datko, K. (2011). The high cost of youth sports. Available: http://money.msn.com/saving-money-tips/post.aspx?post=673566d4-b94f-4f33-a1bf-39fb416498f4

Diamond, J. (1997). *Guns, germs, and steel: The fates of human societies.* New York: W. W. Norton & Company.

Doorey, N. A. (2012). Coming soon: A new generation of assessments. *Educational Leadership, 70*(4), 28–34.

Dweck, C. (2006). *Mindset: The new psychology of success.* New York: Ballantine.

Encyclopedia Britannica. (2014). Creativity. Available: http://www.britannica.com/EBchecked/topic/142249/creativity

Engel, S. (2013). The case for curiosity. *Educational Leadership, 70*(5), 36–40.

Erikson, K., Drevets, W., & Schulkin, J. (2003). Glucocorticoid regulation of diverse cognitive functions in normal and pathological emotional states. *Neuroscience and Biobehavioral Reviews, 27*(3), 233–246.

Fang, F. C., & Casadevall, A. (2013). Why we cheat. *Scientific American Mind, 24*(2), 31–37.

Felling, C. (2013). Hungry kids: The solvable crisis. *Educational Leadership, 70*(8), 56–60.

Garner, R., Brown, R., Sanders, S., & Menke, D. J. (1992). "Seductive details" and learning from text. In K. A. Reninger, S. Hidi, & A. Krapp (Eds.), *The role of interest in learning and development* (pp. 239–254). Hillsdale, NJ: Erlbaum.

Geary, D. C. (2011). Primal brain in the modern classroom. *Scientific American Mind, 22*(4), 44–49.

Gladwell, M. (2008). *Outliers: The story of success.* New York: Little, Brown and Company.

Goodwin, B., & Miller, K. (2012). For positive behavior, involve peers. *Educational Leadership, 70*(2), 82–83.

Greene, R. W. (2009). *Lost at school: Why our kids with behavioral challenges are falling through the cracks and how we can help them.* New York: Simon and Schuster.

Grimes, P. W., & Rezek, J. P. (2005). The determinants of cheating by high school economics students: A comparative study of academic dishonesty in the transitional economies. *International Review of Economics Education, 4*(2), 23–45.

Gunnar, M. R., & Cheatham, C. L. (2003). Brain and behavior interface: Stress and the developing brain. *Infant Mental Health Journal, 24*(3), 195–211.

Guskey, T. R. (2011). Five obstacles to grading reform. *Educational Leadership, 69*(3), 16–21.

Jensen, E. (2005). *Teaching with the brain in mind* (2nd ed.). Alexandria, VA: ASCD.

Jensen, E. (2009). *Teaching with poverty in mind: What being poor does to kids' brains and what schools can do about it.* Alexandria, VA: ASCD.

Jensen, E. (2013). How poverty affects classroom engagement. *Educational Leadership, 70*(8), 24–30.

Johnson, D. S. (1981). Naturally acquired learned helplessness: The relationship of school failure to achievement behavior, attributions, and self-concept. *Journal of Educational Psychology, 73*(2), 174–180.

King, L. A., King, D. W., Fairbank, J. A., Keane, T. M., & Adams, G. A. (1998). Resilience-recovery factors in post-traumatic stress disorder among female and male Vietnam veterans: Hardiness, postwar social support, and additional stressful life events. *Journal of Personality and Social Psychology, 74*(2), 420–434.

Kohn, A. (1994). Grading: The issue is not how but why. *Educational Leadership, 52*(2), 38–41.

Larmer, J., & Mergendoller, J. R. (2012). Speaking of speaking. *Educational Leadership, 70*(4), 74–76.

Lupien, S. J., King, S., Meaney, M. J., & McEwen, B. S. (2001). Can poverty get under your skin? Basal cortisol levels and cognitive function in children from low and high socioeconomic status. *Development and Psychopathology, 13*(3), 653–676.

Lupien, S. J., Parent, S., Evans, A. C., Tremblay, R. E., Zelazo, P. D., Corbo, V., Pruessner, J. C., & Séguin, J. R. (2011). Larger amygdala but no change in hippocampal volume in 10-year-old children exposed to maternal depressive symptomatology since birth. *Proceedings of the National Academy of Sciences.* Available: http://www.pnas.org/content/early/2011/08/08/1105371108.abstract

Marano, H. E. (2003). Procrastination: Ten things to know. *Psychology Today.* Available: http://www.psychologytoday.com/articles/200308/procrastination-ten-things-know

McLanahan, S. (2004). Diverging destinies: How children are faring under the second demographic transition. *Demography, 41*(4), 607–627.

McLeod, S. (2011). Keynote presentation at NESA Conference, Athens, Greece.

Medina, J. (2008). *Brain rules: 12 principles for surviving and thriving at work, home, and school.* Seattle: Pear Press.

Mitchell, T. R., Thompson, L., Peterson, E., & Cronk, R. (1997). Temporal adjustments in the evaluation of events: The "rosy view." *Journal of Experimental Social Psychology, 33*(4), 421–448.

Moss, C. M., & Brookhart, S. M. (2012). *Learning targets: Helping students aim for understanding in today's lesson.* Alexandria, VA: ASCD.

National Poverty Center. (2013). Poverty in the United States: Frequently asked questions. Available: http://www.npc.umich.edu/poverty/

Nawijn, J., Marchand, M. A., Veenhoven, R., & Vingerhoets, A. J. (2010). Vacationers happier, but most not happier after a holiday. *Applied Research in Quality of Life.* DOI: 10.1007/s11482-009-9091-9

O'Connor, K. (2010). *A repair kit for grading: 15 fixes for broken grades* (2nd ed.). New York: Pearson.

Olson, D. T. (2009). *The American church in crisis: Groundbreaking research based on a national database of over 200,000 churches.* Grand Rapids, MI: Zondervan Press.

Pace, J. L., & Hemmings, A. (2007). Understanding authority in classrooms: A review of theory, ideology, and research. *Review of Educational Research, 77*(1), 4–27.

Pink, D. (2009). *Drive: The surprising truth about what motivates us.* New York: Riverhead Books.

Pletka, B. (2007). *Educating the net generation: How to engage students in the 21st century.* Santa Monica, CA: Santa Monica Press.

Posner, M. I., & Rothbart, M. K. (2000). Developing mechanisms of self-regulation. *Development and Psychopathology, 12,* 427–441.

Pyc, M. A., & Rawson, K. A. (2010). Why testing improves memory: Mediator effectiveness hypothesis. *Science, 330*(6002), 335.

Ratey, J. (2008). *Spark: The revolutionary new science of exercise and the brain.* New York: Little, Brown and Company.

Rawson, K. (2010, October 14). Researchers from Kent State say practice tests improve memory. Available: http://www.kent.edu/CAS/Psychology/news/newsdetail.cfm?newsitem=ABE8CBE1-A887-27DA-5190DF7DA66401BC

Reeves, D. B. (2006a). *The learning leaders: How to focus school improvement for better results.* Alexandria, VA: ASCD.

Reeves, D. B. (2006b). Preventing 1,000 failures. *Educational Leadership, 64*(3), 88–89.

Reeves, D. B. (2010). *Standards, assessment, and accountability: Real questions from educators with real answers from Douglas B. Reeves, Ph.D.* Englewood, CA: The Leadership and Learning Center.

Rice, R., & Bunz, U. (2006). Evaluating a wireless course feedback system: The role of demographic, expertise, fluency, competency, and usage. *Simile: Studies in Media Literacy Education, 6*(3), 1–23.

Rick, S., & Loewenstein, G. (2008). The role of emotion in economic behavior. In M. Lewis, J. M. Haviland-Jones, & L. Feldman Barrett (Eds.), *Handbook of emotions* (3rd ed., pp. 138–156). New York: Guilford Press.

Robinson, K. (2001). *Out of our minds: Learning to be creative.* North Mankato, MN: Capstone.

Robinson, K. (2009). *The element: How finding your passion changes everything.* New York: Penguin Books.

Rshaid, G. (2011). *Learning for the future: Rethinking schools for the 21st century.* Englewood, CO: Lead+Learn Press.

Schmidt, M. V., & Schwabe, L. (2011). Splintered by stress. *Scientific American Mind, 22*(4), 22–29.

Schwartz, C. R., & Mare, R. D. (2005). Trends in educational assortative marriage from 1940 to 2003. *Demography, 42*(4), 621–646.

Seigal, D. J. (2012). *The developing mind: How relationships and the brain interact to shape who we are* (2nd ed.). New York: Guilford Press.

Smith, L. K. C., & Fowler, S. A. (1984). Positive peer pressure: The effects of peer monitoring on children's disruptive behavior. *Journal of Applied Behavior Analysis, 2*(17), 213–227.

Southwick, S. M., & Charney, D. S. (2013). Ready for anything. *Scientific American Mind, 24*(3), 32–41.

Texas Education Agency. (2011). TEKS Curriculum Framework for STAAR Alternate. Available: http://www.tea.state.tx.us/student.assessment/special-ed/staaralt/frameworks/

Tomlinson, C. A. (2013). Fairy dust and grit. *Educational Leadership, 70*(5), 85–86.

Villa, R. A., Thousand, J. S., & Nevin, A. I. (2010). *Collaborating with students in instruction and decision making: The untapped resource.* New York: Corwin.

Wiliam, D. (2011). *Embedded formative assessment.* Bloomington, IN: Solution Tree.

Wiliam, D., & Black, P. J. (1998). Inside the black box: Raising standards through classroom assessment. *Phi Delta Kappan, 80*(2), 139–148.

Zhao, Y. (2012). *World class learners: Educating creative and entrepreneurial students.* Newbury Park, CA: Corwin.

INDEX

Note: Page references followed by an italicized *f* indicate information contained in figures.

ABOUT THE AUTHOR

Myron Dueck is a vice principal and teacher in School District 67 in British Columbia, Canada. He has previously taught in Manitoba and on the South Island of New Zealand. Over the past 17 years of teaching, Myron has had experience in a variety of subjects in grades 3 to 12. As a teaching and administrative leader, Myron has been a part of district work groups and school assessment committees that have further broadened his access to innovative steps taken by others. He has presented his student-friendly assessment procedures to fellow educators in British Columbia, California, Idaho, Kentucky, Nevada, Oregon, Texas, Washington, and Greece. Recently, Myron has presented in both Los Angeles and Chicago at the ASCD Annual Conference and has twice been published in *Educational Leadership* magazine.

Related ASCD Resources: Assessment

At the time of publication, the following ASCD resources were available (ASCD stock numbers appear in parentheses). For up-to-date information about ASCD resources, go to www.ascd.org.

Online Courses

Assessment: Designing Performance Assessments course (#PD11OC108)

Print Products

Advancing Formative Assessment in Every Classroom: A Guide for Instructional Leaders Connie M. Moss, Susan M. Brookhart (#109031)

Assessment in the Learning Organization: Shifting the Paradigm Bena O. Kallick, Arthur L. Costa (#195188)

Checking for Understanding: Formative Assessment Techniques for Your Classroom Douglas Fisher, Nancy Frey (#107023)

Classroom Assessment and Grading That Work Robert J. Marzano (#106006)

DVDs

Formative Assessment in Content Areas (3-disc set; #609034)
Giving Effective Feedback to Your Students (3-disc set; #609035)

For more information: send e-mail to member@ascd.org; call 1-800-933-2723 or 703-578-9600, press 2; send a fax to 703-575-5400; or write to Information Services, ASCD, 1703 N. Beauregard St., Alexandria, VA 22311-1714 USA.

WHOLE CHILD
TENETS

1 HEALTHY
Each student enters school healthy and learns about and practices a healthy lifestyle.

2 SAFE
Each student learns in an environment that is physically and emotionally safe for students and adults.

3 ENGAGED
Each student is actively engaged in learning and is connected to the school and broader community.

4 SUPPORTED
Each student has access to personalized learning and is supported by qualified, caring adults.

5 CHALLENGED
Each student is challenged academically and prepared for success in college or further study and for employment and participation in a global environment.

THE WHOLE CHILD

The ASCD Whole Child approach is an effort to transition from a focus on narrowly defined academic achievement to one that promotes the long-term development and success of all children. Through this approach, ASCD supports educators, families, community members, and policymakers as they move from a vision about educating the whole child to sustainable, collaborative actions.

Grading Smarter, Not Harder relates to the **engaged** and **challenged** tenets. *For more about the ASCD Whole Child approach, visit* **www.ascd.org/wholechild.**